Light in Darkness

Light in the Darkness

A History of Lightships and the People Who Served on Them

DR LIAM CLARKE

AMBERLEY

This book is dedicated to my father Arthur Clarke, a former Irish lightship man who served on many lightships about the Irish coast (1907–77).

Dr Liam Clarke

First published 2016

Amberley Publishing
The Hill, Stroud
Gloucestershire, GL5 4EP

www.amberleybooks.com

British Library Cataloguing in Publication Data.
A catalogue record for this book is available from the British Library.

ISBN 978 1 4456 4658 9 (print)
ISBN 978 1 4456 4659 6 (ebook)

Typesetting and Origination by Amberley Publishing.
Printed in Great Britain.

Contents

Foreword

This publication is welcome as it illustrates the experiences and hardships of the ordinary lightship man since the 1730s. It took a certain kind of seaman to man the lightships, one who could stand the loneliness of life on a stationary vessel not far from family and friends. Most lightship men in the British Isles came from seafaring families living close to the sea in local ports. Nearly all of these men, before joining the service, had served on deep-sea boats. Many of the small local coastal communities that these men originated from were in rural areas such as the Kent, Essex and Norfolk counties in England and Wexford and Waterford counties in Ireland. These communities had long histories of seafaring. Many had dockyard and boat-building traditions which declined over the years. As the marine business changed many local men looked for jobs nearer home. With little prospect of work at sea, these experienced seamen sought employment in the lightships and lighthouses about the British Isles. All of them braved the terrifying storms and gales away from families and friends during their lonely spell 'aboard', keeping navigation safe for fellow seafarers. What a welcome sight the Trinity House or Commissioners of Irish Lights relief tenders must have been to these men, with the promise of some time ashore with their loved ones.

Some parts of these islands provided a higher proportion of lightship men than others. One such port and county is that of Wexford in south-east Ireland. So many Wexford seamen served the Commissioners of Irish Lights and formed such a large part of the crews of individual vessels that they were known as the 'Wexford Navy'.

Apart from the hazards of storms and hurricanes, war brought extra danger from mines, submarines and attacks from the air. Many in the Irish and Trinity House service lost their lives during war. In later years the radio-telephone was a wonderful addition both for safety at sea and communications between men and their families. The use of helicopters to relieve lightships and lighthouses also made life safer for those who may have been injured or taken ill. They could easily and quickly be taken off for treatment. Sadly, in a way, while technology was improving the life of the lightship men, it was also contributing to their demise. Automation arrived and all is no more; the lightships, manned and unmanned, have been removed and replaced by automatic buoys or lighthouses that are now also unmanned.

I am so glad that Liam Clarke has undertaken to write this book, setting down a record of these forgotten men who endured hardship and risk to their lives to guide shipping from the perils of rocks and sandbanks around the shores of the British Isles. The story of lightships and the men who worked on them is one of service to others without much thought for their own safety. His telling of the history of the service in my home county was particularly welcome to me as it has not been told before. The story of the 'Wexford Navy' was repeated in fishing and seafaring communities about the British Isles wherever men went to sea.

Though not a historian myself, I was pleased to have been invited by Liam to pen this forward to a book recording a way of life (now gone forever) that has been close to my family for generations. It's a connection for me with my forbears who, since the late 1700s, have been associated with guiding mariners who have sailed about these coasts.

IN SALUTEM OMNIUM

Jack Higginbotham
Wexford 2015

Acknowledgements

This book has been many years in preparation, and many people have provided me with information and materials. It is the product of many meetings and discussions with lightship men, seafarers and museum staff who all told of their experiences and recollections of life on the lightships. Their support and encouragement motivated me throughout this long period. Unfortunately space does not allow me to mention all of them, but I offer them all my warmest thanks for their help.

Having been born in a small seaport that provided many lightship men to the service and having experienced the departure of my father every few months to serve on board lightships has given me some insight into the personal experiences of lightship families. I cannot recollect any of these families talking about their fears for their loved ones during bad weather or storms, but I remember a strong sense of community and mutual support in times of trouble.

My wife, Jane, has played a vital role in encouraging me to write and complete this book. She accompanied me on visits to lightships and archives taking notes and giving me a fresh impartial insight into the lightship service. Without her support, this book would not have been completed.

I would also like to acknowledge the special support I have received from Jack Higginbotham, whose family have served in the lightship and lighthouse service for many generations. Jack was gracious and generous in giving his time, expertise and materials. Other seafarers who gave me their time and knowledge were: Jack O'Leary, for materials and photographs and allowing me access to the archives of the Wexford Maritime Museum; Dr Andrew Lane, curator of True's Yard, Fishing Heritage Museum, Kings Lynn; Neal and Captain McCleane; Ger. Lawlor, and finally Liam Gaul, for his suggestions on the script.

The author and publisher would like to thank the following people for permission to use copyright material in this book. Credit and acknowledgements are given below and also after the caption to each photograph:

EvaK (http://www.gnu.org/copyleft/fdl.html). East Goodwin.

Copyright © 1988–2009 K. Krallis SVıXV – Own work (CC-BY-SA-3.0.). (http://creativecommons.org/licenses/by-sa/3.0). *Nore* lightship.

David (http://creativecommons.org/licenses/by-sa. https://www.flickr.com/
    photos). *Sula* lightship.
Giuseppe Milo (http://creativecommons.org/licenses/by-sa).
Giuseppe Milo (https://www.flickr.com/photos/giuseppemiol). Poolbeg
    lighthouse.
Ian Simons (http://creativecommons.org/licenses/by-sa). *Roaring Middle*
    lightship.
Ewan Monro (http://creativecommons.org/licenses/by-sa. https://www.flickr.
    com/photos). The *Spurn* lightship.
Harwich and Dovercoat (http://creativecommons.org/licenses/by-sa. https://
    www.flickr.com/photos/harwichs). The *Sevenstones* lightship.
Harwich and Dovercoat (http://creativecommons.org/licenses/by-sa.
https://www.flickr.com/photos/harwichs). The Trinity House tender, *Patrica*, 2007.
Ben Salter (http://creativecommons.org/licenses/by-sa). The lightship *Juno*.
Timweather (Public domain via commons https://commons.wikimedia.org/
    wiki/File:North_carr_light_ship_1988). *North Carr* lightship.
Martalnn MacDlomhnall (http://creativecommons.org/licenses/by-sa).
    Fog signal.
Portaferry – Past and Present (https://www.facebook.com/portaferrypast). The
    last crew on the *South Rock* lightship.
Roger (http://creativecommons.org/licenses/by-sa. https://www.flickr.com/
    photos/victuallers). Trinity House Leith.
Reading Tom (http://creativecommons.org/licenses/by-sa. https://www.flickr.
    com/photos/16801915). Trinity House Newcastle.
Mark S (Own work) [CC BY-SA 4.0 (http://creativecommons.org/licenses/
    by-sa/4.0)], via Wikimedia Commons. The *Varn* lightship.
Jack O'Leary, Jack Higginbotham, Dr Lane, True's Yard Musem, Rob Denby
    and Neal McCleane.

Every attempt has been made to seek permission for copyright material used in this book. However, if we have inadvertently used copyright material without permission or acknowledgement we apologise, and we will make the necessary correction at the first opportunity.

Throughout the story of lightships their relationship with the lifeboat service stands out as one of great mutual respect. The lifeboat service was a crucial organisation in supporting the lightship service and saved many lives. However, the lifeboat service also supported the light shipman in many other important ways by carrying out vital routine jobs, such as bringing them ashore when ill or after experiencing accidents and also to be with close family when they were ill. In recognition of their selfless service to all light shipmen, the author's royalties from this publication will be donated to the RNLI.

CHAPTER 1

The Contribution of the Lightship to Safety at Sea

So to the night-wandering sailors, pale of fears,
Wide o'er the watery waste a light appears,
Which on the far-seen mountain blazing high,
Streams from some lonely watch-tower to the sky.

Illiad xix

Introduction

Many books have been written and stories told about lighthouses and the men who manned them, but far fewer about the more hazardous life on a small stationary vessel guarding dangerous areas where the erection of a lighthouse would have been impossible. In rough weather the lighthouse was the more comfortable and safer place, but the men who served on the lightships would have had a very hazardous and uncomfortable time during the winter months. Lightship men were always willing to risk their lives to warn of danger or rescue seamen whose ships were in danger. As Dr Johnson commented, 'Life in a ship is like life in a prison with the chance of being drowned', but this was even more so on a lightship.

The contribution of the lightship to safety at sea has largely gone unnoticed because of its position offshore and being out of sight of the general population. They were invisible except to those who depended upon them, the passing seafarers. A ship that had no engine and did not go anywhere would appear to be of little of interest, but the lightship was the exception. They were literally floating lighthouses with a beacon and a fog signal used to guide mariners and prevent shipwrecks. As floating aids to navigation, they were usually moored in deep water or over dangerous sands and shoals, or positioned on lonely barren stretches of often turbulent water. The men who served on the lightships led hazardous and isolated lives. Lightships had to be manned 24 hours a day, seven days a week and a good lookout kept at all times and in all weathers. In bad weather the lightship had to just sit it out tied to a large anchor on the seabed. 'When other ships fled on the wings of terror ...' to seek refuge in harbour 'the lightship merely lengthened her cable ... and calmly awaited the issues, prepared to let the storm do its worst, and meet it with a bold front.'[1] In the days before radio communication and electronics, lighthouses and lightships offered the only hope a mariner had of completing a safe voyage.

It took a special kind of person to work on a lightship, one who possessed patience, courage and the willingness to place themselves in potentially dangerous conditions for the good of others. The crew came from a merchant seaman background and were expected to be experienced and dedicated mariners on appointment. They needed a full knowledge of seamanship and many had years of deep-sea experience. They were also selected for their reliability, but it was their dedication to the job which was most important and many stayed in the service for years until retirement. For most it was a family job and in many instances generations of the same families saw service on the lightships.

All lightships about the Irish and United Kingdom coasts are now automated and unmanned, which is why it is very important that the life and experiences of the brave men who manned these vessels in the past should be told. Most have died and few remain to tell their courageous tales.

The *East Goodwin* lightship: unmanned, automated and powered by solar energy. (Eva K.)

Ships that do not go anywhere

It was one of the ironies of working on a lightship that the crew spent months at sea, often in sight of land and their homes. The crew would, for the duration of their tour of duty, see nothing but the endless expanses of sky and sea for days on end in a small but well-built craft ceaselessly bobbing up and down on the swell. Nothing was more welcome to the crew at the end of their time on station than the sight of the relief vessel approaching with a fresh crew, provisions and stores. Sometimes, however, the weather was so rough that it was impossible for the relief tender or a small boat to approach the lightship. On these occasions crews were not relieved for many weeks when they resorted to consuming the last of their emergency rations and fresh drinking water.

The job of the lightship was to provide a constant reference position for navigators aboard other vessels in the area and warn them of dangerous rocks or sand banks. Occasionally lightships drifted off station in severe weather, as did the Irish lightship *Coningbeg* in January 1862, dragging her anchor 4½ miles off station. She was for some time thought lost with all hands. Lightships have broken their moorings and as a consequence whole crews have been lost. Others have even been hit by meteorites, bombed, machine-gunned and sunk with their crews.

Early lightship in rough weather. Note the round day marker on the main mast to indicate that she is on station. (Author's Collection)

A lightship swings round during tide changes to face the opposite direction, and in many cases in a strong tide the vessel would list over as much as 45 degrees during this turnabout, but their job was to stay in a given spot come what may. This was important during the most dangerous period of all, when the fog descended and visibility was poor. In fog it was impossible for approaching vessels to be aware of the lightship until the last moment, thus being unable to avert a disaster. Many were run down and sunk because of their positions in very busy sea lanes. Vessels steered for the light and some were unable, at the last minute, to keep clear, having misjudged the strength of the tides or because of inadequate lookouts or poor seamanship. The *East Goodwin* lightship was often struck by other vessels in fog, as was the *Knock*, *Tongue*, *Kish* and *Arklow,* and vessels in the Humber estuary.

The Royal Commission that inquired into the conditions of lights, buoys and beacons in 1861 heard evidence from the Master of the *Sevenstones* and *Coningbeg* lightships, who argued that the most exposed stations were not in effect the most dangerous or disagreeable. The great length of chain required to anchor these two vessels in deep water made them easier to ride than in situations where the sea was shorter, the water shallower and the current stronger such as the Arklow, the Owers or the Humber stations. The Master of the *Humber* lightship, who had crossed the Atlantic sixty times, stated that he had never experienced a more 'nasty' a sea as on the River Humber.

Relieving the *Tongue* lightship at night. (Author's Collection)

Marking danger by manned lightships

The idea of marking danger by manned lights, when first put forward in the early 1700s, was not accepted as a very sensible idea by the establishment. But these early attempts were so successful and welcomed by seafarers that they became permanent – British and Irish authorities used any old hulk as lightships. For a number of years they were only small vessels, converted smacks or coasters, ballasted for stability, carrying a single mast on which would be a light consisting of two ordinary ship's lanterns lit by candles. The lightship *Nore*, the first lightship, was converted from a small trading sloop about 40 feet long and displacing about 50 tons. It was a relatively flat-bottomed vessel that would have bobbed about like a cork in the shallow waters of the Thames estuary. The crew were accommodated in a shelter created on the deck, which was open to all the elements – especially during bad weather. The roar of the wind and the sound of the fog signal at regular intervals would have made sleep near impossible. These first lightships were very crude affairs compared with the later vessels that had lights of 40,000 candlepower or more. Lightships varied in their design and size according to the demands of their station. Some were longer than others. The Irish lightships were generally longer and of more sharper or pointed design than those about the English coast. Many were set with an aftersail to enable them to ride more easily.

The *Dudgeon* lightship, 1736, with two candle-powered lights on her yardarms. (Author's Collection)

Life aboard a lightship

Life aboard a lightship was a dreary and lonely existence, sometimes within sight of land. Listening to and watching life on the nearby coast, which for some was their home, was depressing for many. To hear no sound but the wind, waves and the mournful bleat of the fog horn that conveyed to other vessels the message of imminent danger intensified the feelings of isolation and loneliness. British or Irish lightship men were not allowed to take their family or wives on board, unlike some Australian lightship men who were permitted to take their families aboard for long periods. Because of the isolated position of these vessels, some wives and children served on board with their husbands for over a year at a time.

Lightships were uncomfortable to live in at the best of times with cramped quarters, the ever-present pitching and rolling, and the constant danger of collision from passing ships. In the early nineteenth century the crew lived, cooked, ate and slept all together in one large bare fo'c'sle. In these conditions it was difficult to keep provisions fresh before the introduction of fridges in the twentieth century. Each member of the crew was expected to be self-reliant and responsible for providing his own food and provisions, and all had to take turns at cooking and preparing meals. In bad weather food was difficult to prepare; in heavy weather the galley was dangerous to work in due to the violent motion of the ship. Pots and pans were often flung about, accidents were not a rarity on lightships and in the years before wireless it was common for help not to arrive for days after the incident. It was only when a passing vessel had brought news

The *Alarm* lightship stationed at the Bar in the Mersey estuary. Built in 1912, she was withdrawn in 1961 when she was replaced by a new vessel, the *Planet*. (Author's Collection)

to port that some crew member was very ill that help would be provided by a local lifeboat or Trinity House vessel.

Despite the negative image of life on a lightship, men endured as they felt that they were contributing to the good of others. One lightship man wrote at the end of the nineteenth century:

> This is the best job I have ever had, and I will be glad to stick to it. When I think of my past experience, though, it seems awful. You have no idea how monotonous it gets when the weather is bad. Everything about the ship gets damp and cold and how she does roll. Day and night and night and day the never-ending movement keeps up. Now it is on one side and now on the other. Now she pitches up and now she pitches down. Then something gets the matter with one of the lamps and you have to go aloft in rain and darkness while the whole world seems swinging beneath you. The days drag on so that you forget all about the calendar and can only wonder what is going on in the world that is so near and yet so far. But when a fog comes up and the bells and whistles are going day and night, then our troubles will begin.[2]

The galley on the lightship *Sula*. This vessel was built in 1960 at a cost of £124,128 and served on a number of stations about the Irish coast. She was decommissioned in 1965. (Author's Collection)

LV22, built in 1967. Once moored on the Cross Sand, East Goodwin, Seven Stones, Wolf Rock and St Gowan stations. (Author's Collection)

Others, however, saw beauty at times when aboard the lightship:

> The lightship's utter isolation from other parts of the world is, from certain points of view, a great hardship, but from others it has its advantages. When there is a heavy sea running, the view of the ocean as one 'lays off' in a warm sun is unrivalled. The proximity of the rips and shoals gives the scene a beauty entirely its own. On every shoal there glistens at regular intervals the white curve of a huge breaker. Sunsets can be witnessed from the deck of this vessel which, if faithfully reproduced on canvas, would be pronounced the gorgeous offspring of the artist's imagination. I remember one evening when the sun vanished beneath a bank of fog, permeating it with a soft purple light and edging it with a fringe of reddish gold. Right above it the sky melted from a soft green into the lovely blue that still lingered from the glorious day. Overhead the clouds were shipped out in shreds of fiery yellow, while in all directions around the ship was an undulating expanse of rose-colored sea. Gradually the colors faded away; the creaking of the winches, as the crew raised the lanterns, broke upon the evening silence; two pathways of light streamed over the waves.[3]

The *Kentish Knock* lightship with her lantern lowered to the deck for cleaning. This vessel was run down a number of times. (Author's Collection)

CHAPTER 2

Safety at Sea: the Dangers of Early Navigation

The beacon of hope that soothes his sorrows past and marks the home that welcomes him at last.

The Ancient World

The need for dependable aids to navigation can be traced to the beginnings of maritime commerce. Since early man took to the sea, he was always looking for landmarks to recognize and help him to determine where he was. Going to sea today is dangerous, but in earlier times it was even more so. Seafarers had very primitive boats and had no way of knowing where they were once out of sight of land. They therefore tended to keep within sight of the coast, recognising geographical features on the shore to guide their way. Some features were more readily recognisable than others, especially buildings, trees and tall constructions. These seamarks could only be seen during daylight, and attempts to provide early lights as aids to navigation were primitive and easily extinguished in bad weather by the wind or rain. During the hours of darkness seafarers were better off in the open ocean, where the stars would provide direction. Out at sea they were far from the dangerous rugged hidden dangers of coastlines, sandbanks and submerged reefs. The trained and experienced seafaring eye could spot the swirling waters associated with hidden dangers during daylight, but it was soon realised that lights shown on the shore could be used to help mariners navigate safely during the hours of darkness.

Mention is found in the literature of Europe and the Near East of aids to navigation, some of which were natural phenomena such as fires, trees and tall buildings, including windmills and church steeples. Other navigational aids are mentioned in the Mediterranean area, which were used during the hours of darkness, such as towers surmounted by fires. Shores in this area are prone to severe heavy seas, so it is not surprising that this is where we find the first mention of the lighthouse as an aid to navigation. The first written reference was made by the classical poet Lesches in the seventh century BC, referring to a building which stood at Cape Sigeum, or Sigeion, at the north-west of the Troad region of Anatolia. It was located at the mouth of the modern Karamenderes river, the famous Hellespont. This lighthouse predated the celebrated light tower commissioned by Ptolemy II of Egypt, which was started in 261 BC and finished about forty years later. The Pharos of Alexandria was one of the seven wonders of the ancient world and, when complete, it was the tallest building in the world except for the Great Pyramid. It was situated on the island of Pharos to help guide ships into the harbour at Alexandria. It may also have been used for the defence of the harbour itself.

The Pharos lighthouse was approximately 450 feet tall. The lowest level was 100 feet square and 240 feet high. The second level had eight sides and was about 115 feet tall. The third level was a 60-foot-high cylinder, which had an opening at the top to allow a space where a fire burned to light the way for vessels during the hours of darkness. It was also thought that there was a large mirror inside, possibly made of polished bronze, which projected a beam that allowed sailors to see the light at night far out to sea. The smoke from the fire was also important as it guided sailors during the hours of daylight. Both the beam of light and the smoke could be seen as far as 55 kilometres away. A legend says that the mirror was also used to project a light beam to burn enemy ships before they could sail into the harbour. The tower was still being used as a lighthouse in AD 1155, the Arab geographer Edrisi wrote, 'It is very useful, as it is illuminated by fire night and day to serve as a signal for navigators. During the night it appears as a star and during the day it is distinguished by the smoke.' The tower was damaged by three earthquakes and, after the last one in the thirteenth century, it was abandoned and fell into ruins.

Some types of floating markers may also have existed before the thirteenth century, but the first recorded was at La Compasso de Navigare, located on the Guadalquivir river in Spain. It aided sailors approaching the ancient Spanish ports of Codoba and Seville. The markers were made of hollow wooden casks bound with iron bands and moored with chain and a large stone. Other markers were later recorded in the Vlie river. This primitive buoy was a guide for ships entering Amsterdam harbour.

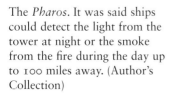

The *Pharos*. It was said ships could detect the light from the tower at night or the smoke from the fire during the day up to 100 miles away. (Author's Collection)

Landmarks in general about the British Isles

On the open sea sailors began to navigate by the sun and stars, but near land these methods were insufficient to identify the dangers lurking beneath the waters, such as the dangerous shoals and sandbanks formed at the mouths of the main rivers and estuaries. The tide's constant movement places great deposits on the sandy bottom of the sea and costal inlets, which then evolve into shifting mounds and ridges of great danger. In some larger estuaries, deposits of mud and sand are also laid down by the tributaries running into it. These sand banks or shoals are usually intersected by deep water channels which are covered and hidden by high tides and cannot be distinguished from open water. On parts of the coastline, dangerous rocks and reefs could also prove fatal to ships and crews. Seamarks were often used to identify the position of these dangers, pointing out the navigable channels and directing vessels to safe havens. The Romans built lighthouses around the coasts of Europe to warn of these dangers, but they were usually used only to aid sailors entering harbours and as a defence against raiders. A number still exist as ruins around the English coast today. One of the most famous is located within Dover Castle on the south coast of England. This lighthouse, erected to a height of 80 feet, was built to guide ships across the English Channel by the conquering Romans.

Landmarks and beacons in general included every kind of terrestrial object that might assist the mariner in steering his course. The spire of a church, the tower of a ruined castle, a windmill on a height, an isolated tree, or even a rock. Two fortifications at Dartmouth harbour appeared as landmarks on sea charts earlier than the seventeenth century. Other types of landmarks can also be found described in early charts, such as the old church at Chichester on the south coast of England. A church tower could be visible above other buildings

The remains of the Roman lighthouse at Dover dating from around AD 465. This lighthouse denotes the early importance of Dover as a port. (Author's Collection)

Reculver twin towers. An imposing landmark, the twin twelfth-century towers of the ruined church were purchased by Trinity House to preserve them as a seamark. (Author's Collection)

or headlands for many miles out at sea. One such was the twin towers named Reculvers, 'The Church of the Two Sisters', which stands on the Kent coast near Birchington. A monastic foundation was established in AD 679 and the church was built later, around 1100. The two towers were repaired in 1500 by Benedictine nuns, which led to them being called 'the Sisters'. Trinity House later realised the importance of keeping Reculvers in repair as a seamark and purchased the towers in 1810 to preserve them as aids to navigation. When the towers were later blown down, about 1814, Trinity House replaced them with a wooden structure at a cost of £1,260 'to render the towers sufficiently conspicuous to be useful to navigation'.[4] The site was eventually handed over to the Office of Works in 1925 for preservation.

The earliest reference of a request made to the Corporation of Trinity House for the erection of a seamark was by Sir John Barker at Woodbridge, who wanted to erect a beacon on his own lands in 1683. His petition was eventually granted but Trinity House later took responsibility for most seamarks about the British Isles. They also assumed the authority for warning mariners when seamarks had been damaged or removed. A *Notice to Mariners* in December 1824 stated that the seamark, the windmill at Freshwater, Isle of Wight, had burnt down.[5]

Earliest recorded manned light in the British Isles

A provision in the Newcastle Trinity House Charter granted permission to build two light towers at the entrance to Shields harbour. One light marked the entrance to the harbour and the second was positioned nearby upon a hill. Both lights were to be maintained during the hours of darkness. Later, in 1566, the government recognised the importance of such seamarks and introduced penalties for destroying or interfering with them:

> Forasmuch as by the destroying and taking away of certain steeples, woods, and other marks standing upon the main shores adjoining to the sea coasts of this realm of England and Wales, being as beacons and marks of ancient time accustomed for seafaring men, to save and keep them and the ships in their charge from sundry dangers thereto incident, divers ships with their goods and merchandises in sailing from foreign parts towards this realm of England and Wales, and specially to the port and river Thames, have by lack of such marks of later years been miscarried, perished and lost in the sea, to the great detriment and hurt of the common weal and the perishing of no small number of people.[6]

Any person found destroying a seamark was to be fined £100, no small penalty in those times, and even worse still the offender was to be considered an 'outlaw'. This legislation emphasised the importance of the safety of shipping to the economy of the country.

Sections of the British Isles coastline such as the Goodwin Sands, the Thames estuary, the Wash, the coast of Cornwall and port of Dublin, have always been recognised as being particularly dangerous to shipping. Some local landowners maintained seamarks, but the system proved inefficient in such dangerous waters. Lighthouse projects were often rejected by both Elizabeth I and James I on the grounds of national security. The argument was that lighthouses could assist enemy shipping at a time of war, and the only effective means of protecting the nation was to extinguish them. This assumption later proved to be wrong, when the cost of replacing lost or damaged shipping threatened the Crown purse and almost bankrupted many shipowners and merchants.

Hook Head lighthouse off the coast of Wexford

One of the earliest attempts to establish a safe light in the British Isles was on the south-east coast of Ireland at Hook Head. It is a very ancient structure and is undoubtedly the oldest continuous light in the British Isles. The first written record dates from about 1247, but local tradition and early Christian records state that a monk, Dubhan, maintained a primitive beacon here as early as the fifth century. It functioned as a warning light for the local seafaring population and for those sailing up river to the important medieval port of New Ross. It would have been a rude structure of stone, earth, and timber built to a suitable height so as to be seen some miles out at sea.

The structure that stands today was built by Raymond, son of William Fitz Gerald of Pembrokeshire, one of the invading Norman lords in 1170. William Marshall, Earl of Pembroke, developed the light further when he established a port in the town of New Ross approximately 30 km upriver. In order for his new port to be successful and for ships to safely reach their destination, he had a 36-metre-high tower built at the entrance to the harbour at the Hook. The first map of the area shows the lighthouse functioning by 1240 and looked after by a small group of monks, Canons Regular of St Augustine, who lived in a monastery nearby.

Many ecclesiastical lights were abandoned at the dissolution of the monasteries as the funds to maintain them were lost. The monks most likely left the tower of Hook in the mid-1500s at the dissolution of the monasteries, but, as this was a very important light, the monks were replaced by the first lighthouse keepers. Because of the disturbed state of the country in the mid-seventeenth century, the light fell into disrepair. In 1671, a new, but still coal-burning, lantern was installed on top of the tower to replace the old beacon and by 1684 the building was again referred to as a lighthouse. In 1704 it was later described,

> Lighthouse at the Tower Hook of this harbour was 140 steps to the top, and above that a large oval lanthorn, glazed, very much in want of repair, and to make the light serviceable an alteration should be made in the light or lanthorn wherein the light was kept. The lighthouse stood in the most convenient part of the harbour's mouth, and was formerly kept by Henry Loftus, Esq. who employed a person who was a smith, and allowed him only 12 barrels of coals yearly to keep up the light, which was no manner of use, &c. It was the opinion of the most knowing men of those parts that the light being once put into sufficient repair could not be kept with less than 200 great barrels of coals every year, at a cost of 30l., and that 40l. per ann. should be given to a careful person to look after it, with two servants to blow up the fires.[7]

Hook lighthouse is one of the oldest working lighthouses in the world. The tower stands four storeys high and its walls are 4 meters thick. The original building still survives, incorporated into the existing construction. (Author's Collection)

In 1728 the local landlord, Henry Loftus, attempted to extinguish the light because of a dispute over the rent. He refused to renew the lease unless the rent was increased from £11 per year to £200, and gave notice that the light would be extinguished on 29 September 1728. A number of petitions were submitted to the House of Lords by local shipowners, and it seems that the threat was not carried out. On 31 March 1734, the king issued instructions to the Commissioners of the Revenue to take on the lease of the lighthouse in case the son of Nicholas Loftus might be 'obliged to let the said light out and to convert the said tower to other uses.' Coal fire was finally abandoned in 1791 when a whale oil lantern, 12 feet in diameter with twelve lamps, was installed.

In 1810 the lease of the lighthouse changed from private hands to the Port of Dublin Ballast Office, who spent £4,281 14s on maintaining it during the years 1811–13. The chimneys broke at a rate of 150 to 200 a year and used on average about 830 gallons of oil each year. Whale oil continued to be used until the lights were installed in 1871, lit by gas manufactured nearby. The first official lighthouse keeper employed by the Ballast Board was a Daniel Kereven, who held the post for fifty years. In 1863, the Commissioners of Irish Lights changed the lights from Catoptric to a Dioptric. During work to complete this changeover, workmen found a large bed of cinders, the remains of the coal fires used until 1791. In 1899 the tower was still held under a lease by the Commissioners of Irish Lights, who paid a rent of £100 a year to the Marquess of Ely. Paraffin was first used in 1911, along with a clockwork mechanism to change the light from fixed to flashing. This mechanism had to be wound up every 25 minutes by the keeper on duty. Finally, in 1972 electricity became the power source and light-sensitive switches were installed to control the lantern. The tower became

Hook Head lighthouse is now fully automated. (Author)

unmanned and fully automatic in 1996. Only one other medieval light was ever established on the Irish coast at nearby Youghal, Co. Cork.

Early lights on the English coast

The monk Venerable Bede, writing between 673 and 735, commented on the name of the Isle of Thanet in Kent, referring to it as the island from the Foreland's blazing lighthouse. In the medieval period many communities considered it their duty to build seamarks or lights to warn seafarers of dangerous coasts. While monks may have tended to lights, not all were built by them. For example, St Catherine's oratory on the Isle of Wight was erected by a rich merchant to fight ex-communication by the Pope. The merchant, Walter de Godeton, purchased numerous barrels of wine from the local wrecking community at St Catherine's. Despite the principle of 'Custom and Descent', where salvage from shipwrecks was considered the lawful right of the people, the Pope considered that, because the wine had been destined for the Catholic Church, the salvage was an act of plunder and therefore sacrilegious. In penance to the church, Walter de Godeton was forced to build St Catherine's oratory to provide a 'chanting priest' and to establish 'a light for the benefit of mariners, to be lit every night for ever'.[9] From 1314 until the dissolution of the monasteries in 1534, the family of Walter de Godeton kept the oratory lit. As early as 1427 a beacon light near the Spurn Head on the Humber estuary was maintained by a hermit.

One of the most famous medieval lights was exhibited from the top of the church on St Michael's Mount in Cornwall. This light was established around the middle of the fourteenth century on the church standing on its island based off the fishing port of Marazion. Ecclesiastical lights were also shown in Scotland, the best known being at Leith near Edinburgh from 1522, while the last known light erected by a religious order in Scotland was at Aberdeen in 1566.[10]

Some early ecclesiastical lighthouses were built on the approaches to the very busy English Channel. These lights used wood fires as the source of illumination and as wood became less plentiful, owing to the depletion of the forests, coal was used and continued to be used for a very long time. After coal, candles were used, later oil and eventually in 1859 electricity was installed at the South Foreland lighthouse. With the increasing number of ships lost along the Newcastle to London coal route, Trinity House in 1609 established at Lowestoft a pair of wooden towers with candle illuminants.[11] During the reign of King Charles II a lighthouse was also placed on the North Foreland to warn shipping of the danger of the Goodwin Sands. This structure was in effect a half-timbered farmhouse with a glass lantern on the roof. The building was destroyed by fire in 1683. Illuminants improved in 1782 with the circular-wick oil-burning Argand lamp, the first 'catoptric' mirrored reflector in 1777, and Fresnel's 'dioptric' lens system in 1823.

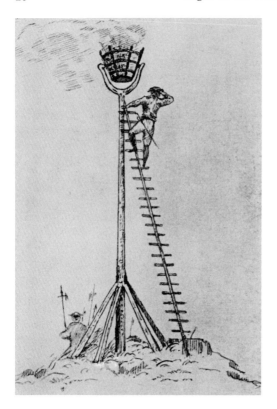

Two types of early light beacons, which would have been manned during the hours of darkness to warn passing vessels of danger. These were in effect no more than a weak light at best. In bad weather resin was thrown on to the light to increase the brilliance. (Author's Collection)

CHAPTER 3
Trinity House

Those poor old dull fellows.

Samuel Pepys

The Trinity House of Deptford, Stroud

An understanding of the role of Trinity House in the development of safety at sea is crucial to understanding the history of lightships. For the past 500 years Trinity House has been instrumental in, at first hindering, their development and, eventually, promoting their use worldwide.

What was 'The Trinity House of Deptford Stroud'? The Fraternity of Trinity House is one of those guilds, partly religious, partly secular, which from ancient times have existed in Britain for the support and regulation of different crafts. In the Middle Ages there certainly existed fraternities under the dedication of the Holy Trinity in some of the larger and important ports, from which have originated the various charitable guilds of seafarers. Some may have been established by King Alfred the Great (c. 849–899). It is also thought that Archbishop Stephen Langton (c.1156–1228) inaugurated the London guild, because of the custom of wrecking and pillaging vessels during the period of King John's reign (c.1167–1216). Langton was determined to put a stop to this custom, so he 'organised in London a corporation of godly disposed men who, for the actual suppression of evil disposed persons bringing ships to destruction by showing false beams, do bind themselves together in the name of the Masters and Fellows of Trinity Guild, to secure from the dangers of the sea … and to build proper beacons for the guidance of mariners'.[12]

The old guilds were religious in character and designed for the mutual benefit of their members, creating their own type of insurance against calamity and hardship. It was self help at its best and Trinity House at this time, as an organisation, inspired confidence and acquired authority to establish regulations for the navigation of ships and the government of seamen. It was, therefore, a tested and approved capacity, which eventually resulted in the granting to it of a charter by King Henry VIII in 1514.

For over a hundred years before Henry VIIIs charter, the organisation had existed in the form of a voluntary association of the 'shipmen and mariners of England'. The only record existing to substantiate this are two graves of Trinity Brethren in Leigh church in Essex: Richard Haddock, who died in 1453, and Robert Salmon, who died later in 1471. The organisation had also owned almshouses and a hall at Deptford, on the Thames estuary, which acted as its headquarters.

Perhaps as far back as the twelfth century, the parish church of Deptford was for many years closely linked with Trinity House when it was associated with the Guild of Mariners. Until the 1500s Deptford was a sleepy little fishing village favoured by shipping because of its deep water and shelter during prevailing winds. The parish church, St Nicholas, was also known as the 'Admiral's Church' after King Henry VIII chose Deptford as the site for one of his naval dockyards in 1513. The fact that Henry's charter in 1514 included provision for a chaplain and for the conduct of divine services in the parish church points to charitable and religious beginnings. Letters patent were also granted to Trinity House, on 20 May 1514, giving rights to oversee pilotage on the Thames and for the maintenance of the almshouses at Deptford.

The reason why Trinity House was launched under the patronage of the Holy Trinity is lost in antiquity. Some argue that the charters were incorporated by King Henry out of love and devotion towards the Holy Trinity. Under the charter it became 'The Master, Wardens, and Assistants

Trinity House almshouses and guildhall, built in 1670 near St Nicholas church, Deptford, Stroud. (Author's Collection)

St Nicholas church, Deptford, Stroud, 1790. St Nicholas parish includes the old maritime settlement and dockyard on the River Thames. (Author's Collection)

of the Guild, Fraternity, or Brotherhood of the most glorious and undivided Trinity, and of St. Clement in the Parish of Deptford-Stroud in the County of Kent.'[14] The first Master of Trinity House was Sir Thomas Spert, who was also Master of King Henry's two great ships *Henri Grace a Dieu* and *The Mary Rose*. He later became Comptroller of the Navy. Some years later a famous early 'Elder Brethren' was one Sir Henry Mainwaring who was twice elected Master of Trinity House despite having been a convicted pirate. Mainwaring also advised the crown against granting pardons to pirates, even though he himself had received one. Oliver Cromwell later sacked him from his position in Trinity House in 1642.

In 1566 an Act of Parliament, the Seamarks Act, enabled Trinity House 'at their wills and pleasures, and at their costs, [to] make, erect, and set up such, and so many beacons, marks, and signs for the sea … whereby the dangers may be avoided and escaped, and ships the better come into their ports without peril.'[15] Queen Elizabeth I later granted a coat of arms to Trinity House in 1573 with a motto *Trinitas in Unitate* meaning 'Three in One', which is believed to refer to the Holy Trinity. The 1566 Seamarks Act also granted powers to Trinity House to erect seamarks at their own expense but later, in the first quarter of the seventeenth century, Trinity House and the Crown were in dispute as to which of them had exclusive rights to grant patents to erect lights. Trinity House eventually won the battle in 1616. However, it was later agreed that the king could also grant patents for the building of lighthouses thus increasing revenue to the Crown. Subsequently many patents were granted to private individuals by the Crown. For example, Sir John Killigrew was granted a patent to place a light at the Lizard despite objections from local wreckers who saw their livelihood destroyed. In 1672, after representation from some northern cities, patents were granted by King Charles II to erect two lights at Spurn Point, a request supported by Newcastle-upon-Tyne Trinity House.

Many grants were also 'conferred on certain high officers of government in remuneration for services, and to other persons who were in confidence and favour with the Monarch'.[16] Trinity House had only itself to blame for this situation having not supported the development of lights. The Brethren had shown no desire to protect their privileges and to therefore act in the best interests of seafarers; by 1609 Trinity House had established only four lighthouses. Whormby, a Trinity House employee, attempted to defend the actions of Trinity House in 1746. He himself stated that he had obtained his post as clerk to Trinity House by patronage stating that he had been elected to the post 'by the favour and firmness of my worthy friends'. In 1615 the Privy Council had allowed a private individual, Edward Howard, a cup bearer to the king, to build a private light at Dungeness. The expense of building and maintaining the structure was to be paid for by a levy on passing vessels. Members of Trinity House had also used their influence to obtain patents for private individuals to build lighthouses, a behaviour which led Samuel Pepys to observe that even Trinity House itself had grown corrupt. Pepys commented in 1683 on the evils of having lights owned by and for the profit of private men and not for the good of the public or the relief of poor seamen and their families. Private patents changed hands over the years through inheritance or were sold for a profit. The lack of any oversight and the inconsistency in standards found between various providers and their failure to update and invest in new technology was a concern to seafarers and merchants. This situation eventually led to calls for change.

The granting of patents to private individuals, a system which had been abused, led to calls for a parliamentary committee to examine the excess earnings and abuses attached to the practice. By 1836 the Crown's ability to grant patents had been extinguished and the sole right was transferred to Trinity House. Powers were also granted to allow them to buy out the rights to all existing lights by compulsory purchase. The total cost of purchasing all the patents from private individuals was £1,182,546, which in 2015 would amount to £99,333,864.

The Court of Trinity House

Under its first constitution, the Court of Trinity House was comprised of one Master, four Wardens and eight Assistants – a total of thirteen. This number had strong connotations with the Holy Trinity, literally 'three in one'. The composition of the court was raised in number by the charter of King James I in 1604 from thirteen to thirty-one, a number still retaining the digits one and three, the extra eighteen being called Elder Brethren. Although members had always been known as Brethren, a title derived from the old Brotherhoods, this charter was the first to refer to Elder and Younger Brethren, terms which still survive today. Younger Brethren were admitted at the pleasure of the court, but had no function in the court except to vote in the election of the Master and Wardens.

By 1746 the aims of Trinity House were:

The art and science of mariners; to examine into the qualifications, and to regulate the conduct of those who take upon them the charge of conducting of ships; to preserve good order, and (when desired) to compose differences in maritime affairs; and, in general, to consult the conservation, good estate, wholesome government, maintenance and increase of navigation and sea-faring men; and (withal) to relieve decayed seamen and their relatives' and to 'regulate the Pilotage of ships in the King's streams.[17]

Trinity House was in a strong position to carry out this work of overseeing the granting of pilot's licences having its guildhall and almshouses at Deptford near the naval dockyard. This was also the base where outgoing ships were provided with a pilot.

The move from Deptford to London in 1660

To be nearer the centre of power, the king, shipowners and other merchants, the corporation moved from Deptford to the City of London in 1660, establishing a base in Water Lane. When in the late 1700s the building proved too cramped for proposed improvements, the corporation bought land at Tower Hill on which a new Trinity House was built between 1793 and 1796. This building was subsequently burnt down and later rebuilt. Later, by 1798, newer and much larger headquarters had been built on land at Tower Hill. The Tower Hill building was severely damaged in the Second World War but rebuilt in 1952, retaining the 1790s facade.

The Trinity House Corporation moved to Old Water Lane in the City of London in 1660. This house was destroyed in the Great Fire of London in 1666 and by fire again in 1714. The rebuilt house gradually fell into disrepair and by the 1790s it was determined that the headquarters should move to the current site on Tower Hill. (Author's Collection)

Trinity House, pilotage and national security

Ancient records refer to 'the policy and necessity of keeping the channels
secret; hence foreign vessels were never permitted to enter the river
without a Loadsman or Pilot'. Pilotage is the art of taking a vessel from
one place to another in sight of land and providing ships with safe passage
into rivers and harbours or through dangerous waters. Most pilots were
usually experienced men with particular knowledge of local waters, but a
number of inexperienced seafarers had begun to offer their services as pilots
with disastrous results. In 1513 a group of mariners associated with the
navigation of the Thames informed the king of the lack of suitably qualified
mariners as pilots. They petitioned the Crown for a licence to regulate their
appointment and training, as many seamen who assisted in pilotage were
inexperienced and easily tempted to make money from wrecking. These
young inexperienced men were unwilling 'to take the labour and adventure
of learning the shipmen's craft on the high seas.' It was pointed out that there
could be grave consequences if this practise continued as it was dangerous to
allow 'foreigners, including Scots, Flemings and French, the opportunity
to learn the secrets of the King's streams.'[18]

The Crown, concerned about the dangers of allowing foreigners to learn
the secrets of the king's streams, declared that no ship could enter or leave the
Thames without a pilot. James II later made provision that pilots were to keep
secret the channels and shoals, and were to be punished if they transgressed by
imprisonment and a fine. He introduced a penalty of £20 to anyone operating

As the Water Lane headquarters fell into disrepair, a new building was started in 1793 at
Tower Hill and completed in 1796. This building was damaged in 1940 and later rebuilt to
its original design. (Author's Collection)

as a pilot without licence from Trinity House. He also stated that in order to 'keep channels wholly unknown to aliens and strangers of other nations'[19], Trinity House was to be given power to prevent any alien or stranger from serving in any English ship or vessel coming 'into or going out of the River Thames ... with a penalty of forty shillings, for the first offence of any Master who should employ them.'[20]

The scandal of life appointments and Trinity House's inability to regulate pilots

In 1608 Sir Robert Cotton, a Member of Parliament, highlighted the scandal of making life appointments to Trinity House. This practice resulted in mismanagement and letting out of revenues at far less than their true value for profit.[21] Trinity House had also been failing to carry out the overseeing of pilots on the Thames, which led to many complaints about their toleration of unlicensed pilots. 'Aliens' had been allowed to practice as pilots; in fact, Trinity House had gone as far as to object, in 1634, to two proposals to make the pilotage of 'alien' shipping compulsory. Writers argue that if Samuel Pepys, who had served as Master of Trinity House, had written an account of Trinity House it would not have been 'a flattering one, for while he was always a staunch and influential upholder of the privileges of the Brethren, he was by no means blind to their shortcomings. Even the Trinity House', Pepys grumbled on one occasion had 'grown corrupt or useless' and he had even called them 'the old dull fellows'. In the late seventeenth and early eighteenth centuries the Brethren of Trinity House had often come under attack for their inaction and negative attitude. They had been accused of trying to keep the amount of money they spent on dinners and socialising out of the account books for fear people might think that they were spending money that should have gone to poor seamen and their families. Free accommodation and provisions had also been offered to Brethren staying in London.[23]

In the 1730s there was a further a hint of possible corruption when the corporation exchanged all of its very valuable plate for less valuable items. This, in the view of an Elder Brethren in 1929, could 'only be regarded as a grave error in judgement; the value of the articles exchanged would today be priceless'.[24] Records of Parliament in 1732 show that the proceedings of the Commissioners of Trinity House were under scrutiny by Parliament itself, as members were thought to have concealed the organisation's true accounts, resources and advantages gained by members.[25] These criticisms were the impetus for a book, written in 1746 by Whormby, which set out to defend the actions of the Brethren and as a rebuttal against the many accusation of corruption made against the corporation at this time.[26]

Societies known as Trinity House, Newcastle, Dover, Hull and Leith in Edinburgh

There are also other organisations known as Trinity House. There is no evidence to suppose that the four other Trinity House societies, that of Hull, Newcastle, Dover and Leith, were ever dependent upon Trinity House London, but there is much evidence of competition between them. Many in London in 1746 were very quick to support Trinity House, London, as the organisation responsible 'for the shipping and seamen of the whole of the Kingdom'.

Hull Trinity House may have had its origins as early as 1357. Whormby, when he visited there, found one document to claim 'one general subscription, dated 1357'. Hull Trinity House was granted a Royal Charter on 5 October 1536 by Henry VIII. The Hull Seaman's Guild, or Trinity House, was formed as a religious guild based about the parish church of the Holy Trinity, Hull, in 1369, and by the middle of the fifteenth century the guild had twenty-four shipmasters. By 1512, Trinity House Hull began to put pilots on ships to bring them safely up the Humber, and in 1585 it placed navigation aids on the Humber estuary. Before the 1580s a buoy, the Canne, had been placed to warn of a sandbank off Spurn Point. Hull Trinity House also later established a nautical school and almshouses in 1746.[28]

Trinity House of Leith, known as the Corporation of the Masters and Assistants of the Trinity House of Leith, owed its beginnings (as did Trinity House London) to the charitable spirit of seafaring men aware of the instability of this occupation. Leith Trinity House dates from before 1500, most likely the year 1380.[29]

The Trinity House of Newcastle-Upon-Tyne had a guildhall which still occupies the same site that was obtained in 1492.[30] Newcastle had petitioned the king in 1685 for a charter, but Samuel Pepys' supporting London managed to steer the request away from the king by forwarding it to Trinity House. No record is available to show what happened to the petition.

Hull Trinity House. The present building was constructed in 1753 and completed by 1759. The original building on the site was occupied by pensioners looked after by Carmelite monks supported by Trinity House. (Author)

Trinity House Leith was a guildhall, customs house and centre for maritime poor relief. In the Middle Ages it served as an almshouse and a hospital. (Roger)

Trinity House Newcastle-upon-Tyne headquarters dates from the fourteenth century. Home to the Newcastle Company of Mariners since the beginning of the 1500s. (Author's Collection)

Trinity House London as a charity

Looking after indigent seamen and their families was one of the main reasons why Trinity House was established, and is possibly the oldest part of their business. Prior to King Henry's charter, the Old Hall and twenty-one almshouses on the Deptford Lower Ground had already been in existence. Monies from levys on vessels entering English ports and fines contributed towards the upkeep of these establishments. Fees collected were applied to the relief of 'decayed seamen, their wives widows and orphans'. In essence the charity contributed to the relief of seamen and their dependants, but it also certificated seamen who had fallen on hard times. This allowed them to beg so as not to fall foul of the

) *Trinity· Alms houses in· Mile End·Road·*

Trinity House almshouses, Mile End Road, built in 1695 by the Corporation of Trinity House on land provided by Captain Henry Mud. The buildings were bombed in 1941. (Author's Collection)

strict vagrancy statutes that had existed from the time of Queen Elizabeth I. In the year 1700, Trinity House had over 1,900 pensioners on their books, and by 1730 the corporation managed ninety-three almshouses. This later increased to 111, and by 1815 the number of pensioners supported had risen to over 7,000.

By 1815 a total of 144 apartments in a number of almshouses were operated by Trinity House at an annual expenditure of £8,000. Eighty-two almshouses were at Deptford and sixty-two at Mile End, in the east of London. As well as accommodation, the occupants of these establishments were allowed two cauldrons of coal a year, suitable clothes, together with thirty-eight shillings a month for a single person and sixty shillings for a married couple. In many cases free medical treatment was offered. For all this support, occupants were expected to attend services at the chapels at Deptford or the Mile End establishments. In the early 1900s in the most well-known almshouse, Mile End, twenty-six Masters were accommodated, nineteen widows of Masters, eighteen spinster daughters of Masters and one pilot. The almshouses also had reading rooms, nursing homes and in addition a medical officer and chaplain were in post. In 1805 a total of £17,769 12s 7p was spent on 'pensions to alms people and monthly pensioners, prisoners of War etc.' The total number of pensioners receiving support was 7,012. By 1920, the total income applied to charitable purposes was £23,702 15s 2p. Trinity House, as a maritime charity, donated over £6 million to charitable causes in 2013.

Trinity House today

Today, Trinity House acts as the General Lighthouse Authority for England, Wales, the Channel Islands and Gibraltar. They have a responsibility to provide and maintain aids of navigation for the safe passage of shipping about the British Isles. To carry out this responsibility they have over 600 different types of navigational aids which are inspected annually. They are also responsible for marking and removing wrecks that are a danger to other shipping. Trinity House also provides navigators and pilots for ships, particularly in northern European waters.

BRITISH EMPIRE
IRISH LIGHTS BOARD

BRITISH EMPIRE
COMMISSIONERS OF
NORTHERN LIGHTS

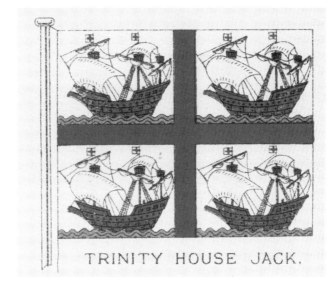

TRINITY HOUSE JACK.

Trinity House, Irish Lights
Commissioners and
The Northern Lighthouse
Board's jacks. (Author's
Collection)

CHAPTER 4

Origins of the Manned Lightship

The lightship a 'curious, almost ridiculous looking craft is among the aristocracy of shipping. It's important office stamps it with nobility. It lies there, conspicuous in its royal colour, from day to day and year to year.

Roman Origins

Lightships are thought to owe their origin to ancient Roman galleys, known as *liburnae*, which provided lighted beacons near harbours to deter pirates. A *liburna* was a type of small galley used by the Roman navy for raiding and patrols. These vessels carried on their mastheads iron baskets in which fire was built serving as a signal when a friendly vessel was sighted. Manned by slaves, they patrolled the Roman coastline and entrances to harbours to guide and protect incoming vessels. However, as ancient sailors tried to not sail in darkness such vessels were of limited importance, and it is not until 1699 that we hear of a 'floating light' again.

Sailors in familiar or in unfamiliar waters have always welcomed the sight of a lightship or other kind of navigational aide. When first put forward in England, the idea of marking danger at sea by a manned stationary vessel was not accepted as a very sound or realistic idea. The first recorded request for such a vessel was in 1699, which did not find much support or encouragement at Trinity House, the body responsible for safety at sea. Concern was expressed that such a relatively small vessel could not be held on station securely by hemp rope attached to an anchor. In the 1600s hempen cables were used to secure anchors and were liable to give trouble by constantly chafing through and letting the ships adrift. A lot of distress and danger was caused if lightships constantly drifted off station. This lack of enthusiasm on the part of Trinity House towards manned lightships caused unnecessary delay in their development until 1731.

The Nore Bank and safety

The Nore Bank is at the confluence of the Thames and Medway rivers, at a key point for finding the entrances to the inner channels of both rivers. The Thames

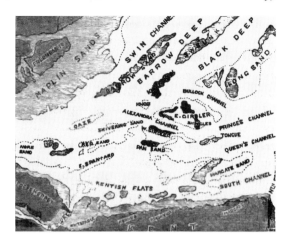

Diagram of the Nore estuary, at the head of the River Thames. (Author's Collection)

estuary is very low lying with extensive mudflats and sandbanks. It was always difficult for vessels entering the estuary to fix their position accurately. In the early 1700s, Medway naval port was a more important port than London. The Nore buoy, placed by Trinity House, served as a seamark and aid to navigation in the estuary, but as it was unlit it proved of little use in bad weather or during hours of darkness.

Early in 1679, a Sir John Clayton proposed a floating light on the Nore Sand instead of an unlit buoy, but Trinity House sabotaged and failed to support the project. Many of Sir John's other patents for safety at sea were also opposed vigorously by private lighthouse owners and Trinity House. However, he did eventually build a lighthouse on the Farne Islands. Later, in 1724, a Captain John Waggett of Yarmouth also proposed the placing of a floating light, but this again was opposed by Trinity House.

Capt. Hamblin's and Mr Avery's lightship, 1731

One Capt. Hamblin caused particular controversy in 1731 with his attempt to establish the first manned lightship on the Nore Bank. For a number of reasons his action was viewed with suspicion by the authorities. They argued that he had positioned the vessel near their existing unlit Nore buoy, which had been placed by them as an aid to navigation during the hours of daylight. Hamblin's proposal was also viewed as a threat by Trinity House to their independence as it affected their attempts to collect revenue. Trinity House was entitled to collect a fee for privately owned lights, but Hamblin argued that his lightship was a new invention, as was his idea to differentiate between different lighthouses, and so not covered by the charter. This attitude of Trinity House can be understood to some extent, considering the history of their attempts to wrestle control of lighthouse and seamarks in general from private developers. The matter was not resolved in favour of Trinity House until many years later.

Robert Hamblin

Who was Robert Hamblin? Robert Hamblin was an experienced and reputable barber from King's Lynn who had been admitted a Freeman of Lynn in the year 1712/13.[32] He married the daughter of a local shipowner and in due time became Master of a vessel engaged in the coastal trade carrying coal from Newcastle to other ports along the east coast of England. He was therefore in a position to judge the dangerous and inadequate manner in which the east coast was lighted. He put forward to the Admiralty, with a Mr Avery, their idea of placing a manned floating light on the Nore Bank. This idea was adopted in 1731. He also placed a second lightship at the Dudgeon Shoal in 1736 at the request of local mariners and east-coast coal traders who often found themselves trapped in easterly winds in the wide area known as the Wash.

Trinity House received the idea of a manned lightship with ridicule: 'How could a barber know anything about lightships?' The clerk to Trinity House Corporation commented on the proposition –

> This patent and description were much wondered and laughed at, nor could those who were not in the project guess at first what was aimed at. Who Capt. Robert Hamblin was, and how qualified, was soon known, and the pompous suggestions of his petition to the King were thought by all to be very unsuitable to him when known. In short, his whole project was looked upon as ridiculous, or as an insolent attempt of bringing all lights under his regulation or control, which no patent could grant in prejudice of prior right.[33]

An early representation of the *Nore* lightship. (Author's Collection)

In an attempt to undermine his proposal, influential friends of Trinity House also put about a rumour that Hamblin was a smuggler. They also argued that as just a Master of a coastal vessel he could not have the relevant experience as 'he was not bred to the sea'.[34] It was held against him that he had not commanded other types of vessels and did not have enough experience so as to give the board an account of the seas about the Scilly Isles or Portland.[35] His status as a barber, and his relative poverty, was also used as a means of belittling his seafaring experience. He had, however, gained a reputation from port owners and seafarers as to his ability as a Master of a vessel with knowledge of the dangers of the east coast.

Hamblin, with Avery, in 1730 also requested a patent from the king for distinguishing one light from another about the coast. He secured the patent for fourteen years from July 1730. Avery, however, was not in a position to finance his ideas. It was said that he was a 'gentleman of infinite projects, who rises in the morning with 100 estates in his head, though most of them slip his pocket.'[36] But between the two of them – Avery with the ideas and Hamblin the money – they managed to obtain enough backing to finance the placement of a manned floating light on the Nore Bank. Both of them had argued that such a vessel was necessary at the Nore sands as ships entering the estuary had been obliged to anchor until day light to pass, which was a great inconvenience to shipowners and often lost them time and money. Often when the weather was bad the delay caused a loss to shipping as they waited to go up the Thames.

The first purpose-built *Nore* lightship. (Author's Collection)

Hamblin advertised his plans as follows,

A prospect floating light near ye Buoy on the Nore Sand, that ships may know how to steer in the darkest Night, between ye said Nore and ye upper Middle: Whereas now they are obliged to anchor till day Light: which is A great Hindrance and Trouble, and sometimes ye Loss of a Ship and cargo. In order to defray ye great Expence of so useful a project ye following prices is hoped will be thought very moderate, and readily comply'd with by all masters, and Commanders of Ships, and ye Vessels; as agreeable to a patent granted by his present MAJESTY to R Hamblin.[37]

The tolls requested were for ships above 200 tons one shilling and six pence each time they passed the light; between 100 to 200 tons one shilling, and for all ships less than 100 tons, six pence. The tolls were collected when the ships entered port.

The vessel was placed on the Nore Bank on 27 July 1731, a newspaper reported on Monday 26 July 1731, the placing of a 'vessel of about 19 tons … to lie at the buoy of the Nore, to the lightships up river; the buoy being not to be seen in dark nights: She has two large Lanthorns at the Topmast head, with two lamps in each lanthorn. Tomorrow she goes to the Nore, and is to be made fast hard at the buoy.'[38]

Early lights

For many years these early lightships were only small vessels such as smacks or coasters, ballasted for stability and carrying a single mast on which would be a light consisting of two ordinary ship's lanterns. A large lantern swung from the yard arm with circular sconces inside it fitted with wax candles. These lanterns could be lowered to the deck for replacement, maintenance or lighting. A very large supply of tallow candles was required to keep the lanterns lighted on the Nore. The two fixed lights – mounted 12 feet apart on a cross beam on a single mast – were reduced to a single light in 1825, but later, after 1855, the Nore had a revolving light. The crew were accommodated in a shelter created on the deck, which would have been open to all the elements – especially during bad weather when the men would have to be on deck keeping watch or attending to the lights. However, these early attempts were so successful and welcomed by seafarers that they became permanent fixtures. The lightship was described by one seaman as 'the beacon of hope that soothes his sorrows past and marks the home that welcomes him at last'.[39]

It was always difficult in those early days to keep the light burning and complaints were made when passing ships could not find the light. A Captain Hallum made a complaint in 1745 'against the light', and it was found that an accidental obstruction on one of the lights had allowed the light to be

Built in 1931, the *LV86* was equipped with a dioptric electric fixed lantern. She served on the Nore Bank between 1941 and 1942 and was stationed at numerous stations between 1931 and 1974. (K. Krallis, SVıXV)

extinguished for only about 30 minutes. The lessee of the Nore light, Mr Cam, agreed to maintain and 'take especial care that a good light be constantly maintained hereafter, to be kindled every evening immediately after sunset and be kept burning till it be broad Day Light next morning.'[40] The security of tenure of a crewman was tenuous in those early days. Mr Cam had offered to replace the crewman responsible for allowing the light to accidentally be extinguished if Trinity House wished. The old *Nore* lightship of 1796 was replaced in 1839 by *LV14* known as 'Old Stormy' until her withdrawal from station during the Second World War.

Support for manned lightships

As the differences between the Corporation of Trinity House and Avery and Hamblin continued, the wider maritime community began to offer strong support for the establishment of manned floating lights. The success of the *Nore* lightship and the continuing support from owners and seafarers forced Trinity House to reconsider its objections to the idea, but it took some time for them to come to terms with the concept. The support from mariners gave Avery the impetus to try to place a similar vessel on the Scilly Isles. However, once again, Trinity House argued that the placing of a lightship on the Nore Bank or anywhere else was an infringement of their ancient legal rights and could not be allowed. The corporation put forward a most unreasonable opinion for the actions of Avery in what they called this 'ridiculous affair'.[41] They exhausted much money and effort to get Avery's and Hamblin's patent overturned. They petitioned the king and among other arguments put forward that the light was 'the dangerous tendency thereof to navigation ... and that the floating lights were no new invention'.[42] However, Trinity House did have to eventually concede that the *Nore* light was 'really useful in itself, and generally approved by navigation; but for him to exhibit a light, and collect money was monstrous'. Such was the attitude of 'the guardians of navigation'.[43] It would seem that the loss of revenue was a more important aspect of this episode than the safety of seafarers. Trinity House was, however, within a short time compelled to admit that the *Nore* lightship was a success and that it proved of great assistance in that part of the Thames. However, the influence of Trinity House and its powerful supporters was in the end too much for Avery and Hamblin, and the king declared their patent void on 4 May 1732.

Avery continued his fight and applied to Trinity House setting out the expenses, about £2,000, that he had incurred in operating and setting up the *Nore* lightship. After much discussion, terms were agreed which allowed Trinity House to be granted a patent for the *Nore* light in 1735. In compensation Avery was granted a lease of the light with authority to collect dues for sixty-one years at a yearly rent of £100. The corporation later obtained the patents for Avery's other rejected projects, including a lightship on the Well. The corporation expressed the opinion of many of the Elder Brethren that, after refusing a later request for a lightship on the Goodwin Sands in 1736, they felt able to offer the opinion that they were not 'fond of them' and were able to say that they 'do not think we shall see any more'. Whormby, clerk to Trinity House, writes that in his opinion the proposals were disastrous for shipping, 'for it is scarce worthwhile to mention a proposal of three lights in one vessel at the Swatch of the Goodwins, which was sent up to Trinity House by two pilots in 1736, but judged trifling' and 'I do not think that we shall have any more. The Trinity House are not fond of them.'[44] Thankfully, how wrong Trinity House and its clerk were.

Trinity House considered a 'floating light' to be stationed at the Sunk Sand in 1796, but it was not carried through because of concerns that it might help an enemy's fleet if they decided to invade. Some early lightships were maintained by Trinity House on behalf of the Royal Navy. These vessels were paid for by the Navy as the corporation did not consider them necessary for ordinary navigation or trade. The Admiralty paid Trinity House the full cost of these vessels, the first being the *Galloper*, £1,800, the *Gull Stream*, £1,500, and the *Bembridge* light, £1,000, a year. The *Gull* marked the deep water passage inside the Goodwin Sands. The first *Gull* was a converted merchantman and she retained her boom and gaff. She exhibited her two lights from her yard arms. In 1836, all three lightships were transferred to Trinity House and became their responsibility.

CHAPTER 5

Lightships: England, Wales and Scotland 1731–1900

Curious almost ridiculous looking craft, was among the aristocracy of shipping. It's important office stamped it with nobility.

The design of early lightships

The first lightships were stationed on the east coast of England, where shoals extend well out from the land and were, and still are, serious obstacles to shipping. They made navigation very dangerous and in many cases fatal to passing ships and lightships alike. The open sea often appears smooth, but underneath lurks shifting sandbanks and strong flowing tides. The deep water passages between shoals are very narrow and difficult to see and navigate when the tide is high. Lightships were also stationed at the entrance to the Bristol Channel, the Mersey, the Humber and near the Scilly Isles. The first lightships sailed to their station, but later ones were towed as they were not self-propelled. Every three or four years they returned to their local Trinity House depot for routine overhaul.

Clean and dirty. This photograph depicts the changeover of vessels to facilitate their cleaning. The vessel on the left is the clean ship and the 'dirty' lightship is being prepared for towing into port for overhaul from the Coningbeg station. (Jack Higginbotham)

Vessels in England and Wales were numbered and changed names according to the station they served on at any particular time. The primary duty of a lightship was, of course, to maintain the light, but they also kept a record of passing ships, observed the weather, and, on occasions, performed rescues.

Lightships were placed on dangerous parts of the coast where it was thought impossible at the time to build a lighthouse. Many unsuccessful attempts were made to build a lighthouse or other seamarks on the Goodwin Sands. Because of the importance of the Thames estuary and east coast approaches, about thirty lightships were eventually stationed in this area. Fewer were stationed on the approaches to other large estuaries such as the Mersey and Humber. The utilisation of the lightship, however, was not restricted to just marking shoals and sandbanks. Clusters of rocks obstructing access to harbours, such as the Daunt Rock outside Cork harbour, rocks off the Saltee islands and off the Sevenstones near the Scilly Isles were also marked by lightships.

These early lightships were described as,

> That curious, almost ridiculous looking craft among the aristocracy of shipping. Its important office stamps it with nobility. It lies there, conspicuous in its royal colour, from day to day and year to year, to mark the fairway between old England and the outlying shoals, distinguished in daylight by a large ball at its masthead, and at night by a magnificent lantern, with Argand lamps and concave reflectors, which shoots rays like lightning far and wide over the watery waste; while in thick weather, when neither ball nor light can be discerned, a sonorous gong gives its deep-toned warning to the approaching mariner, and lets him know his position amidst the surrounding dangers.

The writer carries on his description to say that it is,

> An interesting kingdom in detail. The visitor, standing aft the one mast, sees before him the binnacle and compass and the cabin skylight. On his right and left the territory of the quarter-deck is seriously circumscribed and the promenade much interfered with by the ship's boats, which, like their parent, are painted red, and do not hang at the davits, but, like young lobsters of the kangaroo type, find shelter within their mother when not at sea on their own account. Near to them stand two signal carronades. Beyond the skylight rises the bright brass funnel of the cabin chimney, and the winch by means of which the lantern is hoisted. Then come another skylight and the companion hatch about the centre of the deck.[45]

Lightships eventually became recognisable by their distinctive shape, red hull and elevated lantern. Trinity House vessels were always painted red. Up to the mid-twentieth century, Irish lightships were painted black with a white stripe.

The *Crosby* lightship broke adrift in the Mersey estuary in March 1939 due to the working out of the locking pin in the nut of the swivel pin in the chain cable, which moored the vessel. This was the first and only time this had been known to happen on any lightship. The first vessel placed on this station was in 1840 and it was replaced by an iron vessel in 1842, the *Prince*. (Author's Collection)

Lightships about the Irish and United Kingdom waters had no propulsion to move out of the way of oncoming ships, unlike vessels in other parts of the world. The interior of the early wooden lightships reminded visitors of 'an old wooden fighting ship,' which was 'very roomy, warm and comfortable.' This visitor must have been on board in summer, for these early vessels were usually very wet, cold and uncomfortable in winter and heavy weather. Vessels were altered to accommodate new developments such as heavy lights on their mast and primitive cabins built on deck for the crew. Internally most vessels were made as comfortable as possible but the lightship was built primarily to protect other ships against accident. Some crew called the average lightship a mere hulk but comfort was necessarily subordinate to reliability, serviceability and durability

As the success of manned lightships became evident, colliers voyaging up and down the east coast requested, in 1736, that a manned floating light be placed off the Dudgeon Shoal in Lincolnshire, at the entrance to the Wash. Twelve years later, the Overs Shoal was marked by a floating light to guide shipping bound for Southampton, Portsmouth and the Isle of Wright. Others quickly followed with a vessel placed at the Newarp Sand in 1790. Vessels placed north-east of the Goodwin Sands in 1795 were the first to exhibit three lights, one on each mast, forming a triangle. Other sections of the Goodwin Sands – the Galloper sands and the Gull stream – had vessels positioned on them by the beginning of the 1800s. The *North Goodwin* had one light on each of her three masts in 1795. The four vessels in the approaches to the River Mersey were maintained by the Mersey Docks and Harbour Board until 1973.

Those in the Humber estuary were the responsibility of the Humber Conservancy Board.

The *Formby* lightship of the Liverpool Dock and Harbour Board. The first lightship placed on this station in 1840 was the *Queen*. (Author's Collection)

The *Haisbro* lightship. The lantern on this vessel was lowered each morning to the deck for cleaning and hoisted each evening before darkness fell. This station was later called the *Newarp*. (Author's Collection)

The *Roaring Middle* lightship was stationed in the Wash at the estuary of the Humber river. (Author's Collection)

By the middle of the nineteenth century, lightships were described as short for their,

Length, bluff in the bows, round in the stern, and painted all over, except the mast and deck, of a bright red colour, like a great scarlet dragon, or a gigantic boiled lobster. It might have been mistaken for the first attempt, in the ship-building way of an infatuated boy, whose acquaintance with ships was founded on hearsay, and whose taste in colour was violently eccentric. This remarkable thing had one immense mast in the middle of it, supported by six stays, like the Norse galleys of old, but it had no yards; for, although the sea was indeed its home, and it incessantly braved the fury of the storm, diurnally cleft the waters of flood and ebb-tide, and gallantly breasted the billows of ocean all the year round, it had no need for sails. It never advanced an inch on its course, for it had no course. It never made for any port. It was never either homeward or outward bound ... Its helm was never swayed to port or starboard, although it had a helm, because the vessel turned submissive with the tides, and its rudder, being lashed hard and fast amidships- like most weather cocks-couldn't move. Its doom was to tub perpetually, day and night, from year to year, at a gigantic anchor which would not let go, and to strain at a monster chain-cable which would not snap-in short, to strive for ever, like Sisiphus, after something which can never be attained.

The writer went on to say that the 'curious almost ridiculous looking craft, was among the aristocracy of shipping. Its important office stamped it with nobility.'[46]

A representation of the early *Goodwin* lightship with three lanterns, each hoistable. (Author's Collection)

The design of purpose-built lightships in the nineteenth century

The shape and the construction of lightships in the nineteenth century was very different to the first vessels. The new vessels had to withstand great stresses because of the winds and tides. Initially the lightships were constructed of wood, with lines like those of any other small merchant ship. This design proved to be unsatisfactory for a vessel that was permanently anchored in dangerous positions with strong tides. The shape of the hull evolved to reduce rolling and pounding and to adapt to running seas and the winds that often came from amidships. New hull shapes had to be designed to deal with these stresses and were constructed of a wooden hull on an iron frame, the deck made of teak. Up to about 1900, most vessels were about 103 feet in length with a beam of just over 23 feet and depth of 14 feet or more, but as these vessels became more established, they also became more complex. Two large substantial bilge keels were later placed on either side of the hull to help them ride more comfortably in severe weather. The hull was copper sheathed below the waterline. These new lightships remained on their station for seven years, when they were then brought in and received a thorough overhaul and repair. The vessel always had to be kept clean and the crew also had watch-keeping duties. Later vessels were more strongly built tubby vessels specially designed to ride out easily at anchor. They were moored by their bow, so that they would swing around with the tide.

Mooring the new heavy lightship

The poor design of early mooring systems and the inherent dangers of vessels drifting off station can to some extent account for the slow introduction of the lightship. Mooring early lightships proved problematical as only hemp was available to attach to the primitive anchor. Hemp cables were liable to be destroyed by the alternate action of air and water, and especially by chaffing in rocky anchorage and heavy weather. Iron was suggested as a substitute in 1771, but the idea was not taken up to any extent until the early 1800s. One of the gravest questions connected with the consideration of placing a lightship was whether she was likely to stay where she was put. All seafarers agreed that better no light at all than an uncertain one. The precautions against breaking adrift were consequently very great. Vessels had to be moored in such a manner as to ensure that they remained at their station in all weathers. Many broke their moorings and drifted, but they could manoeuvre by hoisting sail to either run for safety, if in danger, or to move back to their established station. This course of action would be denied to later vessels which, once they broke their mooring, were always in mortal danger as they had neither sail nor engine. At first a number broke their moorings and drifted from their station, but as the methods of construction and the design of mooring cables improved, they became more reliable. When a lightship drifted she was a great danger to other passing ships, who might not realise that she was off station.

Since the beginning of the nineteenth century, anchor cables were made of iron, prepared and toughened to be strong enough to hold a vessel of 600 or 700 tons. Most lightships at that time were only about 160 tons. In narrow channels the moorings consisted of a chain lying along the ground for 1,260 feet, with a 32 hundredweight anchor, in the shape of a mushroom, at each end and a swivel in the centre, from which rose 630 feet of chain as a bridle or veering cable. This passed into the vessel on one side of the bow. In deep-sea channels, a single vertical chain was employed, 1,260 feet long. This chain, lying along the bottom, acted as additional drag upon the lightship when she was driving before the full scud of those terrific seas that rush by from the Atlantic. When she came to the end of her tether, and had to lift it or part from it, it rose in a curve, which spared both the vessel at one end and the anchor at the other.

When a lightship broke adrift she had ground-tackle on board to use in such emergencies, two bower anchors 20 and 15 hundredweight each, with cables respectively 1,260 and 900 feet long. One of these went overboard the moment the vessel was felt to be either parted from her mooring, or to be dragging her mushroom. Sometimes they were brought up instantly, sometimes not for many hours; but if her position had shifted a dangerous distance a red warning signal was hoisted, guns were fired and assistance summoned. The vessel was replaced when it was safe to do so.

Anchor mooring chains at a Trinity House depot yard. (Author's Collection)

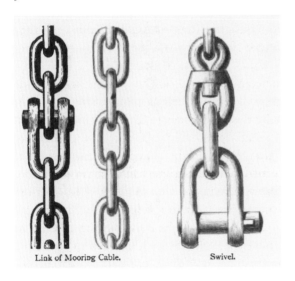

Link of Mooring Cable.   Swivel.

Anchor chains and links. (Author's Collection)

Mooring cables began to be made of iron usually 1½ inches in diameter. To ensure safety, each link was examined before going into service so that it could take a strain of at least 23 tons per square inch. The chains were manufactured in 15-fathom lengths, with a swivel to prevent kinking during use. By the mid-1800s the cables were manufactured and tested in Wales and were made of the best iron. Before being delivered to Trinity House they were exposed to a strain of 80 tons and inspected to see if there was the slightest symptom of weakness. Each lightship was supplied with at least 210 fathoms of chain, and some with as much as 315 fathoms. They were provided with cables strong enough for a vessel three or four times their tonnage. The lightship on the Seven Stones station was moored in 40 fathoms of water and was one of the larger vessels supplied with 315 fathoms of cable, which was changed every four years.

Care of the anchor

The care of the anchor cable was one of the most important duties on board a lightship. It was vital to ensure that the anchor remained firmly embedded in the seabed. It was also important that the cable did not become wrapped around the anchor, particularly when the tide was turning. The cable had to be let out in bad weather and hoved in when the circumstances allowed so that it did not become tangled when it would be liable to break. This all had to be done by hand until powered windlasses were introduced in the 1930s. To prevent chafing of the cables at the hawse-hole by the movement of the vessel, they were occasionally played out a few yards – a process called 'easing the ship'.

Near the bow of the vessel was the anchor windlass which had two large anchor chains, only one of which was connected to the mushroom anchor.

This cable was coiled two or three times about the massive windlass passing through an opening in the rail or bulwarks near the bows and down into the sea attached to the anchor. A most difficult task, with the early hand-operated windlass, was the hauling up of the heavy anchor or adjusting the riding cable. The hand windlasses were operated by inserting a long iron or wooden bar into slots on top of the windlass. It usually took two men to lift each bar. The slots were then cranked up and down to drive a pawl over a ratchet gear wheel. The chain was raised slowly and, as it was usually in bad weather or a heavy sea that this operation was most performed, it could exhaust fit men very quickly. The cable had to be played out during heavy seas to allow the vessel to ride more easily and reduce the strain on the cable. It was not usually the anchor that kept the ship on station but the large amount of heavy cable laid on the sea floor. In good weather this extra cable had to be winched back in.

Since the early nineteenth-century, lightships have used mushroom anchors – named for their shape – which typically weighed 3 to 4 tons, and were just like a common mushroom. The side of the circular head lay half buried in the seabed and usually held the vessel firm. This type of anchor was invented by Robert Stevenson, who used it on his 82-ton converted fishing boat, renamed *Pharos*, a lightship, which entered service in September 1807 near to the Bell Rock off the coast of Scotland. It had a 1½-ton anchor. The effectiveness of these mushroom anchors improved dramatically in the 1820s when cast iron anchor chains were introduced. The rule of thumb was that 6 feet of chain were needed for every foot depth of water.

In the early days the anchor often fouled, but improvements such as the 'Martin's Patent Anchor' held the vessel more securely in suitable stations. The advantage of Martin's anchor was that it was self-canting: the weight of the arms, together with the pull of the cable, pressed their sharp points into the seabed, so that it took hold immediately. It was near impossible to foul it and

A manual anchor windlass on a wooden lightship. The hand windlass was operated by inserting a long iron or wooden bar into slots on top of the windlass. It usually took two men to lift each bar. The slots were then cranked up and down to drive a pawl over a ratchet gear wheel. (Author's Collection)

A later development of the 'Martin's Patent Anchor' on an Irish lightship. (Author)

A motorised anchor windlass on an iron and steel lightship in the 1920s. (Author's Collection)

it stowed much more neatly than any other anchor. There was a second cable on the windlass to be used in emergencies.

In most cases, the cable connected to the mushroom anchor weighed about 2 tons and allowed the lightship to swing with the tide. However, on stations where the channel was very narrow and the lightship had little room to swing, a different method was used. Two mushroom anchors were employed, connected by ground cable lying along the sea bottom. In the centre of this chain, attached to a ring and swivel, was a short chain which was attached to the lightship.

A lightship mushroom anchor. (Author)

This cable could be hove short so that the vessel swung in a very small area. All lightships were supplied with one or two other anchors for use in emergency and also additional lengths of chain. In good weather a short cable is sufficient, but when the sea ran high it was necessary to pay out a long section of the anchor chain so that the ship could ride out the heavy seas. The surplus cable on the seabed, because of its weight, also acted as a spring and prevented straining. The vessel was never allowed to go to the end of her 'tether', which would cause her to pull on the anchor and place a strain on it causing it to break or drag.

What kind of man wanted to serve on a lightship?

One member of a lightship crew answered this question in an eloquent manner:

> When our lights are aloft in the dark nights of winter, many a brave seaman is watching for a glimpse of our friendly light to guide them clear of the rocks and shoals of our dangerous coast. What a dreadful thing it would be for them if our lights round the coast were let go out for only one short hour! How many a poor seaman would be cast into destruction! O may we never neglect to let our light

be burning, for we too are being watched every hour of our life! I pray that my influence may be for good, and I pray that my light may never grow dim.[47]

Working as a seaman throughout the centuries has always been a dirty, hazardous manual job, and life on the lightship was no different. Many of the men who served on the early wooden lightships were experienced seaman who wanted to work near home after years serving on deep-sea vessels. Most, if not all, were qualified 'able seamen' with a Board of Trade certificate. In those early days they spent as long as two months or more on station and just one ashore. Time ashore was not a holiday or free time as they had to work in a nearby Trinity House repair yard or depot.

One writer, commenting on lives of lightship crew in the late 1800s, wrote:

Lonely they are, and you can see their isolated life written in their faces. Riding on the edges, as all lightships do, of the dangerous outlying shoals and sands round our Island, they are witnesses to tragedies which they are unable to avert. It rests with them at fixed intervals to summon the far-off Lifeboats, and it also rests with them to attend all night in wildest winter tempest and blinding snowstorm, the machinery which regulates the motion of each revolving light.[48]

Many individuals had difficulties dealing with the loneliness and isolation of such a long time on board. Some were reported to have lost their 'reason', and ended in a local 'lunatic asylum'. Others died after accidents on board. For example, in 1924 Charles Darn, aged 50, a lamplighter, fell into the hold and was killed.

St Nicholas lightship off Lowestoft. This station was established in 1837. In 1887 the light character was one fixed white light with one red flash every 10 seconds; in 1919, the character had changed completely to show a revolving green light every 20 seconds. Notice the toilet cabin in the stern. (Author)

CHAPTER 6

The Life of the Crew

The men were very respectable.

Why would men wish to work in such a dangerous and lonely occupation? Lives depended on the vessel being shipshape with all equipment in good working order and ready for use in any emergency. Lightships were always maintained to a very high standard and a lot of brass cleaners and gallons of red and white paint were used over the years. Many a house in sea ports where crewmen lived also looked as smart in white paint as the lightship they served on.

Lightships were divided into two classes: 'Offlying' and 'Inshore'. The makeup and number of the crews was decided by which class they fell into. Offlying vessels, usually the largest, were crewed by a Master, or Mate, lamplighters, a cook and nine seamen – a complement of eight crew at any one time being a Master, or Mate, lamplighters and six seamen. Inshore vessels would usually have a complement of six crew. The Master and Mate took turns so that one was always on board. Two lamplighters were also usually on board at any one time. The crew spent two months on station and one month ashore. It was reported in the early 1800s that some individuals, to oblige some of their colleagues, would remain up to six months on board at any one time. By 1850, the lightship man had no other occupation than his professional lightship duties. Crews consisted 'of eleven, of whom four come ashore every month for a month, and are employed in the storehouse at the buoy wharf. The Master and Mate are in command month and month about. Only good seamen are entered.' Individuals could rise from the 'lowest rank to that of Master' rising by seniority. The crew was not a man too many owing to the duties to be performed especially in fog or heavy weather. In some waters crews were busier than others – for example on the Goodwin Sands and the Nore Bank, which were stationed in busy shipping channels.

After two months on board the crew, when relieved, were expected to work in the local Trinity House maintenance depots. Here they cleaned and repainted, overhauled and repaired buoys. They were also on call to work on

Blackwall Trinity House depot and wharf. Trinity House established this depot in Blackwall in 1869. The workshops were built alongside a ship depot that had been on the site since the early nineteenth century. (Author's Collection)

any lightships that came into dock for repair or maintenance. Many resented this unfair system and in 1872 eighteen men refused to go to sea stating they 'had done a hard day's work and would not go till next morning.'[49] Nine men refused to embark on the *Vestal*, the Trinity House relief vessel, on 2 August 1930 to relieve the *Calshot Split*, *Warner*, *Owers* and *Royal Sovereign* and were later reprimanded at an Industrial Court. The men had refused to sail on a Saturday instead of Monday, which would have been a change in their usual practice. The court considered 'whether the men's refusal was justified, and if not what disciplinary action would be fair and adequate in the circumstances.' They lost a year's seniority. This system was eventually replaced in 1937 by the introduction of shore leave for one month with no work responsibilities and time to relax after a difficult six weeks or two months on board.

A typical routine on early lightships

If it were not for the endless round of work on board, the deadly monotony of the life would have been unbearable. Any crew not on watch either slept in their hammocks or carried out other duties below decks in the forecastle. It was the responsibility of the Master to conduct an informal service each Sunday. A general tone of 'decent, orderly and superior conduct' was observed of the crew, that the men were 'very respectable … and supplied with a bible as well as a library of varied and entertaining literature.' Each lightship was issued with several prayer books and a large leather-bound Bible.

The general routine of the duty was:

Sunday; at sunrise the lantern is lowered down into the lantern-house, the lamplighter then cleans the lantern, and trims the lamps ready for lighting the ensuing evening. At 8 A.M. all hands are called, the hammocks triced, and breakfast served. After this, the crew clean themselves, and at 10.30 muster in the cabin for divine service. At sunset the lantern is hoisted, and at 8 P. M. worship is again celebrated in the cabin. On Monday, Tuesday, Thursday, and Friday, the routine is the same, without the service; and on Wednesday and Saturday it is varied by washing of decks and a general cleaning out below. The state of the wind and weather is noted every day at 3 A. M., at sunrise, at 9 A. M., and noon, at 3 P. M., at sunset, at 9 P. M., and at midnight. In foggy weather the gong is beat at intervals of from two to five minutes, both by day and night. The watch consists of two men on deck, the others relieving them at stated intervals. As near as possible to the full and change of the moon, the cable is heaved in short, in order that the shackles and swivels may be examined, and then veered out again.'[50]

The watch

A strict watch was held day and night in all weathers. The watch usually consisted of two men who kept a lookout together on the upper deck. As well as watching out for passing ships or other dangers they had the responsibility, usually the lamplighter, for tending to the light or the fog signal. If any of the watch saw danger, one or both of the carronades would be prepared for firing to warn of danger. One each of these was situated on the port and starboard sides. These were fired to warn passing vessels that they were running into danger, or if they were off course and in danger of running down the lightship. There were usually seven watches in 24 hours. The first watch was from 8 p.m. until midnight. The next was from midnight until 4 a.m., 'the middle watch', and the morning watch was from 4 a.m. to 8 a.m. The 'fore noon' was from 8 a.m. until midday. The afternoon watch was from midday until 4 p.m. and the 'first dog watch' was from 4 p.m. to 6 p.m. The final watch, 'the second dog watch', was from 6 p.m. to 8 p.m.

Men off watch or the 'watch below', meaning that they were not on deck duty, were expected to carry out cleaning and maintenance duties.

Leisure time

When all duties were completed those crew members off duty could spend their leisure time in the forecastle where they made rope mats or rugs, toys, inlaid boxes and ships in bottles. Some also painted postcards, or pictures of their ship; others made small fretwork and marquetry boxes. Many were decorated with a lightship like the one illustrated on page 68. One crew member wrote in 1980 of the skills of lightship men: 'Another aspect that intrigued me was the skill of the men on board: simple men with only a basic education. Yet they could create works of art of the most intricate design from a variety of coarse materials, ships in bottles and bulbs, extraordinarily coloured and shaped rope mats, unusual ashtrays and toys. One man who made brushes of all descriptions used to take hair from local horses but one day was caught in the act and fined £50.'

The ability of the lightship men to entertain themselves when on board was remarked in the early 1800s:

> They are very ingenious fellows. Some of them take canvas, &c. from the slop-sellers, and make it up; others learn shoemaking, and make and mend for themselves and families; some make models of vessels, washing troughs, linen horses, pegs, mats, wheel-barrows, and toys: it is a common saying at Yarmouth. Wait for the relief of a light-vessel, and you can get anything, from a chest of drawers to a penny whistle.[51]

The Master's accommodation

The Master may have had a separate cabin, but the crew all slept in hammocks in the open forecastle. The only toilet on board was an unheated hut on the deck with no running water, just a bucket on a line. On some vessels the Master's cabin had skylight windows that could be opened in warm or fine weather. On each side of the cabin was a bunk with drawers below, with a small cupboard at the head. One bunk was for the Master and the other for the Mate. A curtain could be pulled to provide privacy. This cabin also contained a small coal-burning stove, two chairs, a small table and a washstand. One important job carried out by the Master and Mate was to write the ship's log in which entries were usually made every 3 hours until midnight. None but the Master or Mate ever saw the log.

The captain's cabin on the *Gull* lightship in the late 1800s. (Author's Collection)

The crew's quarters

Much of the space in the early lightship was taken up by storage for oil and crew accommodation. Later, space was more efficiently utilised when engines were introduced to run air compressors. On wooden lightships there were only two decks, the main deck and the lower deck. The crew lived in the forepart of the lower deck. The quarters were small, about 10 feet or so in length, and about 8 feet in width. The deck above was low and some crewmen found it difficult to stand upright. The living quarters were always kept very tidy and clean, as was the entire vessel. Sometimes the crew lightened their surroundings with pot plants and vases of flowers. Just forward of the crew's accommodation were the coal bunkers and, most importantly, the anchor cable locker. The crew's provisions were stored in lockers. There was also provision of a brine locker on board to preserve meat.

Heat was obtained from a small fire in a well-polished grate which kept the quarters warm. Their mess had in it a large table and lockers, which served as seating. The large table usually had a 'fiddle' about the edge which kept the eating implements from falling when the ship was rolling in bad weather. The crew's toilets or 'heads' were placed at the stern on the upper deck. In warm weather a wind-sail was rigged to draw cooler air into the living quarters. This apparatus was a large funnel shaped from a sail. With its wide trumpet-shaped mouth upwards, it was lashed on the deck in such a position that the mouth was towards the quarter where the wind was blowing. The wind entered the wide mouth and swept down the canvas tube.

The crew had to be careful as the ship rolled in very bad weather and accidents often occurred. The Mate of the Scottish lightship *Abertay* was seriously injured when he scalded his face and hands in an accident and had to be taken by a passing fishing boat to port for treatment. When not in use all the eating implements, cups, plates etc. were arranged in a recess, which acted as a cupboard.

The crew accommodation in a wooden lightship in the late 1800s. (Author's Collection)

The wind funnel, which was used to cool the crews quarters in hot weather, can be seen just aft of the main mast on the *Shambles* lightship. (Author's Collection)

Feeding the crew

Writing in 1891, one member of the crew of a lightship described eating arrangements aboard:

Forward on the berth-deck is the cooking-stove and beyond it is the mess-table. The lightship version of dinner under difficulties, familiar to every ocean traveller, is, if anything, a little livelier than the original. The method of keeping the table service in place is, however, somewhat more primitive than that in use on the ocean greyhounds. There are holes in the table into which pegs are fitted, and around each dish and cup is a little fence of these pegs. Sometimes, however, a plate will clear the fence on a running jump and deposit its contents in a dish of quite a different character, the result being a conglomeration mysterious enough to puzzle even a person who has solved the most profound problems of the culinary art. The mainstays of life aboard a lightship are scouse and duff. Scouse is a wonderful commingling of salt beef, potatoes, and onions, with varied trimmings. Duff seems substantially like dumplings served in Yorkshire pudding with a sauce of melted brown sugar. Plum-duff-with-raisons is a great luxury; but often the plums are nothing more than 'Nantucket raisons'—in plain English, dried apples. Now it is easy to imagine the result if a rolling sea causes the scouse and the duff, with its sugary sauce, to fraternize.[52]

The average pay in the beginning of the nineteenth century was about 55 shillings a month, increasing through the higher grades, the Master receiving £80 per annum. They were 'victualled with a weekly allowance of 10 Ibs. of meat, 1 Ib. of suet, 7 Ibs. of bread, 2 Ibs. of flour, 7 Ibs. of potatoes, 1 pint of pease, 2 oz. of tea, 1 lb. of sugar, and may draw Is 3*d* per week in lieu of 3 gallons of small-beer. When on shore, they draw Is 3*d* per day per man in lieu of provisions'.

By the late 1800s, Trinity House lightship crews served under service regulations. Supplies had not changed much as they were provisioned per week as follows: 'meat 8¾lb, bread 7lb, flour 2lb, peas 1 pint, potatoes 7lb, suet 1.2lb, tea 2 oz, sugar ¾lb, butter, ¾lb, beer 3 gallons.'[53] A money allowance in lieu of beer of 19s 6p per quarter would be given to men who did not drink. Before 1891, the Master of a vessel provided provisions for his crew who paid him directly for them. He of course made a profit on this transaction, a situation not un-similar to the Victorian system of paying wages in a local pub, or paying workmen with tokens to be spent only in the factory owner's shop. This abuse was discontinued in March 1891, when each member of the crew was paid 1 shilling and 9 pence a day for food. Each man became responsible for his own provisions and was expected to purchase food ashore for his time on station. The Master of the lightship was granted £10 per annum as a personal allowance to compensate for the loss of profit he had previously made by provisioning his crew himself. This allowance was recognition that Masters had indeed made a profit from provisioning their own crew. As well as the crew members' individual food, the whole crew had to maintain a supply of emergency provisions which could be kept in stock for up to two years. This usually consisted of 'two hundred and sixteen 1lb tins of meat and seventy two 3 lb tins of biscuit' supplemented by blocks of chocolate, sugar and sea biscuits.' This amount was slightly less for vessels with fewer crew.

Fresh provisions were stored on board in wire cages, which helped keep them fresh. The majority of provisions were hard-baked biscuits or preserved salty fish and beef. These were put in tubs called the 'harness-cask' and covered with salt to preserve them. Sometimes passing vessels threw a newspaper, fresh fish or food to the men on board. The crew also supplemented their provisions by fishing, and on at least one occasion, a crew made a pie from twelve-dozen larks that had been captured on one night. Bread was usually baked on board and stored in bread lockers near the galley. Milk came from a tin or, as it was

A lightship man with his provisions coming on board. (Author's Collection)

called, 'the cow with a tin tail'. The cook kept a large cooking-pot on the boil in which there would have been several little netted bags, each one belonging to a different member of the crew. Into this netted bag each crew member put his own chosen food to be cooked.

Relief day

Trinity House steamers visited lightships to change crew and bring provisions including fresh water, coal and oil for the lamps, as well as paint and spares. When going ashore or coming on station, the Master or Mate of the lightship wore buttoned suits and peaked caps with the gilded crest of Trinity House on the cap. Other crew such as the seamen and lamplighters wore jerseys. Relief day was looked forward to by everyone on board as it was a day when crew went ashore to their families and loved ones and new crew took their place. Those left on board would get fresh food, stores, letters, papers and parcels from home. Before the arrival of the relief vessel most of the crew would have spent hours cleaning, polishing and scrubbing the ship. Personal bags, cases and baskets, used to transport stores, would be placed on deck ready to be transferred to the relief vessel.

In the Irish lightship service the provisions were usually packed in large wicker baskets, waterproofed inside and covered outside by waterproof canvas. If it was a calm day the relief vessel could come alongside the lightship, but if the weather was rough stores would have to be transported by small boat between the two vessels. Coal, stores and men would be drenched as the boat

A member of the crew on an Irish Light's vessel preparing to go ashore with his empty baskets in which he had brought his provisions on board some weeks earlier. (Jack O'Leary)

The Trinity House lightship tender *Alert* was used to relieve lightships and lighthouses in the late 1800s. (Author's Collection)

slowly made its way to the lightship. Hook ropes would be lowered from the lightship and stores would be jerked aboard with speed, sent below and packed away safely. In Irish waters the relief was sometimes carried out by small boats from local harbours as well as the larger Irish Lights steamers and tenders.

A young man's account of his first visit to a lightship on relief day

A year or two before the lightships were de-manned, a young temporary lightship man gave a vivid description of his first visit to the *Coningbeg* lightship on the south coast of Ireland.

The relief boat left from Fethard, a small fishing village not far from Hook Head. It was about twelve miles to the lightship and the boat was a small trawler, its skipper a man called Lewis. The day was quite windy. As we reached the open sea we began to pitch and dip into what seemed like unending valleys of blue. I recall the sensation of looking up into the sea, feeling as if my stomach was somewhere above my head! Although I had never before met Lewis, I had the utmost of trust in him. He was a seasoned sailor, or at least looked like one, and surely he wouldn't risk our lives if he didn't know what he was doing. Time has since changed that innocence to cold rationality. Having just passed the Saltee Islands, an impressive natural landmark with its gentle form and natural colours, I caught sight of the 'Coningbeg' – a tiny red speck, formless, an anchored island,

The Trinity House lightship tender *Patricia* used to relieve lightships and lighthouses, seen here in 2007. (Harwich and Dovercoat)

a cocky little thing facing up to the elements with apparent gusto. An Alcatraz to some, maybe; a way of life to others; a possible escape for more. But to me it was surreal, almost spellbinding. The sense of adventure welled up in me more than the waves in the increasingly turbulent sea. The sea was so rough that we had to pull alongside and at a suitable point jump on board. In this way I and the supplies came aboard the lightship, while the liberty crew jumped aboard Lewis's boat and, after a few cordial exchanges, were off running with the waves towards terra firma and the warmth of their family.[54]

The first lightship to be relieved by helicopter took place in 1972 when the *Smiths's Knoll* had its crew changed by helicopter on the 14 October. The transfer was carried out by winching the individual crewmen and provisions to and from a purpose-built platform on the lightship deck.

How difficult was it to provision a lightship in bad weather or fog?

Conditions could become difficult on board when the relief vessel was held up by bad weather. Many Irish and English lightships were particularly prone to this happening as bad weather was frequent on the south-east and south coast of Ireland, the Humber estuary and the Goodwin Sands. On many occasions vessels were not relieved for weeks, crews were often down to their last few rations and quickly running out of fresh water before they were finally relieved. In the mid-1800s a proposed visit to a lightship on the Goodwin Sands, the *Varne*, was successful only after a number of attempts. The graphic account illustrates how difficult it was to get alongside a lightship in heavy weather or thick fog:

> We tried again a fortnight later, in better weather. This time the wind was light, and after making South Foreland, about eight miles from Deal, we stood out for the Varne south-south-west. As we got out a fog came on, and at last it became so

thick that we could barely see the length of the boat. All kinds of ghostly shapes and spectral ships, all manner of imaginary noises and sounds came at us out of that wreathing vaporous fog. We were ten miles from land, and yet we heard the breaking of surf and the whistle of railway engines, and the tinkle-tinkle of a ship's bell. That last sound seemed so real that we all cried, 'Listen', and then it came again. and at that moment right over our head there loomed the great sails and spars of a large ship; but her hull, though not more ten yards off, was absolutely invisible.[55]

Right: A Trinity House steamer relieving a lightship in bad weather. Note the small cutter carrying out the transfer of men and provisions. (Author's Collection)

Below: The *Smith's Knoll* was the first lightship to have its crew changed by helicopter in 1972. (Author's Collection)

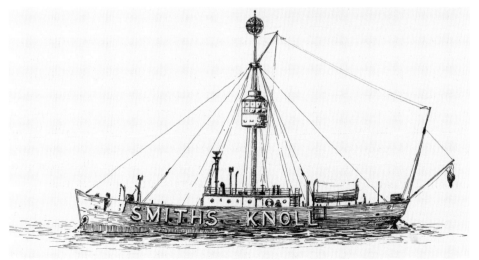

Needless to say they did not find the lightship and returned home more by good luck than seamanship.

At Christmas time each year, weather permitting, the local seaman's mission boat would visit or the lifeboat with local dignitaries on board who would be welcomed. They all came bearing gifts of large turkeys, Christmas puddings, mince pies and loaves of freshly baked bread from the local community. Also, parcels from individuals in the community containing woollies, soap, cigarettes, writing paper etc. were delivered. If it was the local mission boat bearing gifts, a short service would be held on deck before the minister left.

The ship in a bottle was made by a lightship man in the west of England in the first part of the twentieth century. (Author)

A ship in a bottle made by a Wexford lightship man, P. Broaders. Mr Broaders is the lightship man illustrated on page 64 preparing provision baskets for going ashore. (Author)

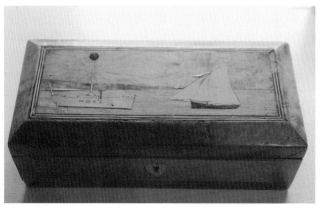

The wooden inlaid box shows the old *Nore* lightship and was made in the later nineteenth century by a lightship man in Kent. (Author)

CHAPTER 7
The Development of the Lights

Right through the centre of this house rises the thick, unyielding mast of the vessel; and the lantern, which is only just a little smaller than its house, surrounds the mast and travels upon it.

Keeping the light on early lightships

The early lightships were conversions of simple small wooden commercial vessels with a lantern placed on each end of the yardarm which was hoisted up just before darkness and lowered each morning for cleaning and repair. The first illuminating lights were of the simplest construction, a small lantern provided with flat-wick oil lamps unaided by optical apparatus of any kind. When candles were used they were prepared on deck and then hoisted into place each evening before dark. These wooden vessels were tossed about in bad weather and it would have been difficult for passing ships to see the light, but this simple attempt to provide a safe aid to navigation proved effective and was also profitable for the owners. By day a large round globe at the top of the mast, or in some cases two or three masts, was visible from every point, but at night the light was raised to identify the vessel and her station. In some cases the heavy lights had to be lowered in bad weather to prevent the lightship being swamped when she moved violently in the heavy seas.

Later lights consisted of groupings of oil wick burners in silver copper reflectors. The number and size of lamps used on individual vessels varied from nine to twenty-four. Good ventilation in the lantern was very important so that heated air escaped freely and fresh air supplied. The lighting apparatus differed from that of the lighthouse in that the lightship was never still and in a rough sea rolled heavily and continuously. This rolling of the vessel was counteracted by swinging the burner and optical apparatus on gimbals. The light was also mounted on ball bearings or rested on a mercury float, which allowed the light to rotate more easily. In the first purpose-built lightships a lantern, usually about 5 feet in diameter surrounding the mast, was arranged so that it could be lowered to the deck during the day for cleaning. In later vessels the lantern was fixed and mounted at the top of a short hollow steel mast. The design was large enough for a man, usually the lamplighter, to enter and carry out cleaning and lighting operations. The lantern was usually octagonal, with eight large panes of glass each a ¼-inch thick. Inside were twelve lamps arranged in groups of three, with each reflector faced with silver. The lights were mounted on a frame and rotated by a weight-driven clock which, in the beginning, had to be wound every half hour by crew on watch. A large clock regulated all the movements of the lantern, and both the clock and lantern had to be carefully watched each night.

To distinguish between different stations during darkness, each vessel's light had different characteristics to differentiate it from other lightships. Some had single coloured lights, others flashed in different combinations. By arranging the reflector at different angles and groupings and changing the gears on the clock, different light sequences could be achieved which identified each station. Light could also be coloured or be made to rotate or flash, which allowed individual lightships to be recognised by their distinctive patterns. For example, the *Bull Sand* vessel had a white fixed light; the *Spurn* a white revolving light at one minute intervals; the *Outer Dowsing* had a red revolving light and the *Sunk* a red and white revolving light every 45 seconds. The *Mouse* had a green light, as did the *East Goodwin*. The *Selkert Light* was red and white, flashing one white one red every half minute.

The invention of the parabolic reflector made individual lightship identification much easier, but the main problem was in keeping the light steady. The solution was to mount the optic above a seat of gimbal bearings counterbalanced with a weight so that the optic would remain upright.

As well as the light that operated from 1 hour before sunset to 1 hour after sunrise, early light vessels were equipped with red (or very occasionally white)

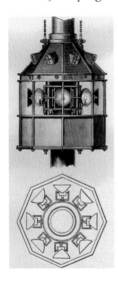

An early hoistable lantern with revolving lights. (Author's Collection)

day markers at the tops of masts, which were the first things seen from an approaching ship. The designs varied with filled circles or globes, and pairs of inverted cones being the most common among them. These were made of wood, hollow and open, with the wood strips painted red on most occasions. A collapsing ball, made of wood and canvas, was always supplied as a substitute in case of accidents or breakages. During the day, each vessel had a different configuration of day marks on one, two or three masts to identify itself from other lightships. The familiar black ball at the masthead served to indicate that the lightship was safely on station. If she was off station for any reason, this ball was lowered. If the vessel was off station during darkness then the lantern was lowered and red lamps were usually suspended to indicate her position and show passing ships that she had drifted from her station.

Right: An unidentified lightship used on the east coast of England in the early nineteenth century. Note the early lights not encased in a lantern. It is reputed to be the vessel that once served on the *Roaring Middle* station. (Dr Lane, True's Yard Musem)

Below: An early depiction of a lightship and illustration of the first type of candle-powered lights used. (Author's Collection)

Raising the lantern

Most days, but not in very rough seas, the decks were scrubbed, repairs were made and painting was carried out. The quarter deck was usually cluttered by the ship's boats painted red. Next to them were two signal carronades, and beyond them the brass funnel of the cabin chimney rose from a skylight. Near this was the winch that raised the lantern to the top of the mast. The mast, on which the lantern was hoisted each evening, ran right through a small house on the deck. During the day it housed the lantern when lowered for repair or maintenance. It took five crew members to man the winch which hoisted the lantern and one other who worked on the block and tackle which supported the lifting process. The lantern rose slowly as it usually weighed over ½ ton. It was hoisted to about 10 or 15 feet beneath the ball at the top of the mast. When the lantern was in place the lamplighter climbed up and connected the lantern with the rod and pinion to the clockwork mechanism which revolved the light by machinery working from below. The gigantic clock regulated all the movements of the lantern and both had to be watched all night. Once the lantern had been hoisted, a single lamp was hung up near the bows 12 feet above the deck to indicate to approaching vessels in what direction the lightship's head was turned.

The lamplighter

The lamplighter was an experienced and important senior member of the crew who was responsible for looking after the lights. Two of them usually served at any one time, as the lantern had to be maintained at all times and in all weathers. Maintenance of the light when not lit was also the responsibility of the lamplighter – he had to clip and trim the wicks, fill the lamps and polish the glass chimneys. The tips of the burners also had to be immersed in boiling caustic solution, which kept them in good order. He had also to polish the reflectors and brasses, oil the joints and wheels of the revolving mechanism and finally clean the glass and windows. The oil room, which was near the Master's cabin, had a lead sink in which the lamps were cleaned on a daily basis and filled. Lockers held glasses, wicks and trimmers, all connected with the lantern. Oil to feed the light was also stored in this room in metal cisterns.

In bad weather the lamplighter's job was particularly dangerous as he had to maintain the lantern when it was hoisted. He had to climb the stays or swaying iron ladder, which could lead over 40 feet from the deck to the lantern – a very dangerous manoeuvre in wild weather. In 1893 Rev. Thomas Treanor, after visiting the *Varne* lightship, commented on the dangers of climbing to the light:

> It is sometimes a formidable task to climb the swaying iron ladder leading from the deck to the great lantern which is fixed at a height of forty feet from the sea.

To clamber into the little iron door in the lantern, crossing somehow the yawning gap between it and the end of the ladder, or to reverse this process in descending requires the natural agility of a monkey, or the skill of a gymnast or sailor. Once inside the reeling motion of the regular flash of the lights, the clicks of the machinery and the roar of the wind, are enough to turn the head, so say nothing of the digestion of the victim.[56]

Amidships on the upper deck stood the lantern house, in which the lantern was lowered each morning into its enclosure to allow the lamplighter to clean the lamps and trim the wicks. The deckhouse in which previously the lamps were cleaned was gradually converted to an enclosed space and used for shelter for those on watch in particularly bad weather. Some of the smaller lanterns did not allow the lamplighter to enter inside the lantern so it was cleaned from the outside.

One description of this activity in 1872 is instructional,

Just beyond is the most important part of the vessel the lantern-house, a circular wooden structure, about six feet in diameter, with a door and small windows, which encloses the lantern, the beautiful piece of mechanism for which the lightship, its crew and appurtenances, are maintained. Right through the centre of this house rises the thick, unyielding mast of the vessel; and the lantern, which is only just a little smaller than its house, surrounds the mast and travels upon it. It is, of course, connected with the rod and pinion by means of which, with the ingenious clock-work beneath, the light is made to revolve and flash once every third of a minute.[57]

The lamplighter cleaning the lowered lantern on the *Gull* lightship around 1900. (Author's Collection)

An early Argand lamp with reflector on a gimbal.
(Author's Collection)

At about half an hour before sunset the lantern was lit and hauled back up the mast by the manual winch. As the lanterns became larger towards the end of the nineteenth century they were lowered just to the roof of the deckhouse or in some instances kept continuously aloft, which meant that lamplighters had to climb the ratlines to clean and service the light.

The oil lamps in the lantern were lit by hand and extinguished in that manner also. Later, tubular tower masts were built with a stairs or ladder construction which kept the lamplighter dry and relatively safe when carrying out maintenance on the light. The first design was an octagonal shape about 5 feet in diameter. Usually eight oils lamps provided light with these lanterns and were ventilated by a number of individual cowls at the top of the lantern to allow the fumes to dissipate. Air was drawn in through ventilators in the base of the walls of the lantern which had to be manipulated so that the lights were never blown out by wind.

The Argand lamp

Over the years the design of the light changed. Aime Argand, a Swiss philosopher, found a way in 1781 of avoiding the nuisance of smoking to which early oil lamps were prone. Aside from the improvement in brightness, the more complete combustion of the wick and oil required much less frequent trimming of the wick. Argand's design featured the incorporation of a hollow cylinder within the circular wick, which allowed air to flow both inside and outside the flame at the upper edge of the fuel-soaked wick. The addition of a cylindrical glass chimney created greater draft, promoting steadiness in the flame by

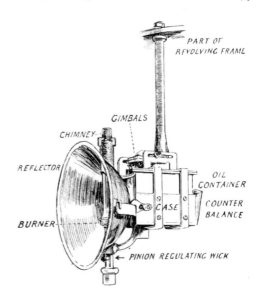

An illustration of the Argand lamp on
the *Gull* lightship at the beginning of the
twentieth century. (Author's Collection)

preventing side draughts. This incandescent vapour lamp used kerosene, which
eliminated the smoke and fumes. Argand successfully obtained a patent for
this lamp while living in England in 1784. Early models used ground glass,
which was sometimes tinted around the wick. The Argand lamp used oil as fuel
supplied by a gravity feed from a reservoir mounted above the burner. The oil
generally used by Trinity House was rape seed oil until the middle of the 1800s
when mineral oil was introduced.

A disadvantage of the original Argand arrangement was that the oil reservoir
needed to be above the level of the burner because the heavy sticky vegetable
oil would not rise far up the wick. This made the lamps top heavy and cast a
shadow in one direction away from the lamp's flame. The parabolic reflector
is thought to have improved the light output of the lamp when placed behind
it, as it could project the beam at least 10 miles out to sea. There is some
disagreement as to who was the first to place parabolic reflectors behind
Argand's lamp to boost and concentrate the output. This combination
represented a considerable improvement over current illumination systems,
and quickly came into widespread use in European lighthouses and lightships.
These first reflectors used on lightships were usually 1 foot in diameter and later
were enlarged to 21 inches.

Light-projecting lens

Without a means of projection, light wasted most of its intensity through
diffusion, but with reflectors light could be directed. An important development
in illumination came in about 1822 when Fresnel invented the refracting or

dioptric lens. His idea was to arrange a bull's-eye lens surrounded by concentric rings of prismatic glass, each ring projecting a little beyond the previous one – the effect was to bend or refract the light into a horizontal beam. The rings were known as dioptric, later further reflecting prisms were added, catadioptrics, which recovered the wasted rays of light in the dioptric system. This design created a bee-hive appearance. Up to about 1895, lights were always of the catoptric type with a number of burners and their metal reflectors. In 1905 dioptric apparatus was installed with a single burner and glass prisms. Electric light was introduced in 1926 and a number of lightships were built with powerful catadioptric electric lights. The *Outer Dowsing* was equipped with electric light in October 1926 and the *Royal Sovereign* lightship in the same year. The *Outer Gabbard* and the *Newarp* were equipped in November 1927. In all these vessels a 3 kw filament lamp was fitted.

The lanterns used to house the lights went through many different designs, each one in turn making for an improvement. Robert Stevenson is credited with the first design for a lantern encircling the mast of a lightship in about 1807. However, models of earlier lightships at Trinity House show vessels with lanterns circling the mast. There may have been a number of people who had the same idea, as is usually the case. Further improvements meant that some of these lights had intensity in the beam of about 20,000 candles. In 1875 the first group-flashing light, showing three successive flashes at 1-minute periods, was installed on board a new lightship moored at the Royal Sovereign Shoals, off Hastings.

A lantern on one of the last manned lightships in British and Irish waters. *The Guillemot* was built in 1923 at a cost of £17,000. She was sold to Wexford Maritime Museum in 1968. She has since been sold and broken up. (Author)

The Royal Sovereign, stationed off Hastings in 1900. This vessel was the first to have a flashing light in 1877. This lightship was withdrawn in 1971 and replaced by an automated light tower. (Author's Collection)

The dangers of fog: when lights are not effective

In the early nineteenth century the only warning that a lightship could give of its presence in fog was by means of sounding a large bell. Later, Chinese gongs were introduced, which were more resonant and penetrative in the thick fog. Guns were also used, generally fired every 10 or 15 minutes during fog. Lightships were later equipped with powerful fog-signal apparatus, which superseded the traditional gongs. These were manually operated reed horns with a pump which raised pressure. The operator would release the pressure to sound the horn at specific periods which identified each individual vessel. Cranking the foot pedal to pump the horn was exhausting work as the operation could go on for days if the fog lasted. In 1915 the fog horn on the *Gull* lightship was,

> Worked by manual labour or should I say by pedal labour; it is blown by working the treadle attached to a tall upright cylinder I saw at the ship's stern. Inside this large cylinder is a chamber for containing air which the working of the treadle forces into it. A little circular dial, like the face of a clock, is fixed outside the cylinder, and on it a set of figures up to '10'. When the treadle is worked a pointer begins to move round the dial, and when the pointer reaches the figure '5' that means that five pounds' pressure of air has been accumulated – enough to give one or two blasts. By the time I had pumped up a pressure of five pounds I wanted a rest of several minutes, for the working of the treadle is not very easy. But had I been on duty on the Gull in time of fog I should have had to keep up working almost continuously for half an hour at a time; for half an hour's work is each man's spell.[58]

A system by which mechanical air compressors were activated by a wheel attached to the lantern clockwork motors was introduced later. Much later fog signalling took the form of a fog-horn, siren or diaphone operated by compressed air, but some of the older fog horns were used up to the middle of the 20th century. Vessels built later in the twentieth century were fitted with three types of fog horns which operated in conjunction with each other, an electric foghorn, a wireless signal and a submarine signal. The main fog signal, the fog horn, was provided by an electric nautophone, the trumpets of which were fixed immediately by the lantern, one forward and one aft of it. A standing manual reed horn was always available in case the electric horn broke down. The fog horn was always turned mouth to windward.

Early fog horn for a lightship in the 1880s. (Author's Collection)

A lightship fog horn. This type of horn could be rotated so that the sound could travel further. (Author's Collection)

When fog came down it was a difficult time for the crew, but it also had its advantages for they were paid extra for each day they had to attend to the fog signal. Each man was paid an extra 2 pence per hour. Fog could last without a break for several days and this extra payment was known as 'fog dust' or 'noise-money'. This system of payment was in some instances abused and as a consequence discontinued later in the early twentieth century.

Marconi's early wireless apparatus

Before the introduction of wireless, lightships could only communicate with other vessels by hand signals or flares. Help could only come if passing vessels relayed on messages when they reached port. In 1894 telephone land lines connected the *Sands Head* lightship on the Goodwins with the shore, a distance of about 5 miles. A telephone similar to those used in the postal service of the time was fitted on the lightship.[59] The first ship to shore wireless communication took place between the *East Goodwin* lightship and the South Foreland lighthouse near Dover, a distance of 12 miles. The *East Goodwin* was equipped with wireless apparatus so that she was capable of calling for assistance. During this experimental period in 1899, the lightship was hit by heavy seas which tore away part of her bulwarks. The men on board were able to report the incident to Trinity House by wireless.

Radio cabin on the *Tongue* lightship, around 1900. This equipment was similar to that used on the *East Goodwin*. (Author's Collection)

In April of the same year the lightship was hit by a large four-masted vessel, the *R. E. Matthew*s. The first lightship man to call for assistance by wireless was Mr Ashby from Kent. Born in 1865, he had entered the lightship service in 1886. He eventually became Mate of the *East Goodwin*. This was the first time that a radio telegraphy signal ever was sent for assistance from a lightship in danger.

Radio cabin on the *Sula* lightship in the 1960s. (Jack O'Leary)

CHAPTER 8

Lightships in the Twentieth Century

These first wooden lightships were very crude affairs compared with the later vessels that had lights of 40,000 candlepower or more.

The last of the wooden lightships

In the late 1900s the job of lightship man was a sought after occupation among seafaring men, particularly in counties such as Kent, Suffolk and Essex in England and Wexford County in south-east Ireland which had a long seafaring history. The Commissioners of Irish Lights and Trinity House paid reasonable wages and allowed many opportunities for promotion to lamplighter, Mate or Master. A crew member could earn up to just over £100 a year, however out of this they would have to feed and clothe themselves when on board.

Up to the mid-1880s a number of wooden lightships had been built for Trinity House; they were usually constructed of an oak frame with teak and elm planking. These vessels were usually small in size, about 100 feet in length and 20-feet breadth, and provided slightly more adequate accommodation than the very early vessels. Wooden vessels gave long service. The *Petrel*, built in 1854 for the Irish Lights at a cost of £3,800, was not taken out of service until 1920, having seen service for over sixty years.

The crew's quarters on these wooden vessels were usually entered by a companionway from the upper deck and were situated below the main deck, fitted with six bunks plus individual lockers. The accommodation was equipped with wooden lockers for the crew's personal belongings such as waterproof clothing and uniform. A galley stove was mounted on a slab of stone situated in the crew dining area with an accompanying fire fender and coal scuttle. For the first time an enamelled iron bath was provided. Meat and dairy products were stored on the upper deck in meat safes and later modern fridges were provided. Each crew member still cooked their own food, but Trinity House now provided cooking utensils.

The *Mouse* lightship, a good example of a wooden vessel. She was stationed near Maplin Sands off the Essex coast. The *Mouse*, while stationed in the Thames, was attacked by German aircraft and replaced by a light buoy in 1941. (Author's Collection)

The Master's cabin, also used by the Mate, was immediately astern of the crew's quarters and offered privacy and more comfort. Two sleeping berths were fitted with storage drawers and space. There was a private water pump and hand basin and an enclosed bath and lavatory. A writing desk was also fitted near the coal stove and a clock mounted on the bulkhead.

The *Varne* lightship was another good example of a nineteenth-century wooden vessel that was in service until well into the twentieth century. Life aboard the *Varne* just before the Second World War was less comfortable than in most lightships of the time, the vessel being over a hundred years old. An ancient hand-winch was still used on the foredeck. Heavy muzzle-loading carronades were positioned on both sides of the deck and also twin tubes for rockets that summoned the lifeboat in time of danger. The only objects on the after deck were the mizzen mast, two lifeboats and the scuttle to the Master's cabin and lavatory. The fo'c'sle was large and roomy but with little head room and contained the crew's mess. Here, the crew stored their belongings and stores and slung their hammocks when sleeping. A bare wooden table ran fore and aft, flanked by well-worn wooden stools. Forward of this table was a large cooking range, upon which there was always a boiling kettle. The whole space was lit by two oil lamps of highly polished brass, and as usual everything was absolutely clean and well maintained.

Iron and steel lightships

In around 1850 lightships began to be constructed of a composite consisting of an iron frame and teak planking. This construction was improved by the introduction in the late 1800s of vessels composed of a steel frame and teak planking sheeted with muntz metal. The Irish lightship which was sunk by a German submarine in 1917 was one such vessel. With the introduction of iron and steel vessels, life began to be more comfortable for many of the crew. The first lightship constructed of iron for Trinity House was *LV40* in 1861. These lightships needed less maintenance than previous wooden ones. In 1903, one lightship built of iron was found free of corrosion thirty years later and had only dry docked once every four years for maintenance. The first composite iron and steel vessel was built for Trinity House in 1906, although the *Fulmar*, costing £6,800, had been built two years earlier for the Irish Lights Commissioners. It was, however, not until 1930 that conditions for the crew improved to any extent on these vessels when they enjoyed a galley, mess room and washrooms. New cabins also replaced the hammocks in the forecastle. Later the deckhouse was enlarged and all of the men were provided with single cabins. On the deck was a lookout shelter in which the steering wheel was also placed which afforded more shelter to the watch in bad weather.

Many of the lightships in the twentieth century were built by Phillip & Son of Noss between 1935 and 1962. During these years they built twenty-nine lightships for Trinity House, five for the Commissioners of Irish Lights and one vessel for the Mersey Dock and Harbour Board. Most of these were manned vessels, but some of the later ones were unmanned and powered by remote electrical and solar power. One of the vessels they built was the ill-fated *South Goodwin*, which was lost in 1954 with all the regular crew.

The iron and steel *Albatross* built for the Commissioners of Irish Lights in 1926

The seventh iron and steel vessel commissioned for the Commissioners of Irish Lights – the first being the *Fulmar* in 1904 – was the *Albatross*, built by Henry Robb of Leith. This vessel came into service in 1926 and was seen as 'an excellent modern example of such a type of vessel'. Her construction was supervised by Captain W. H. Davis, Inspector of Irish Lights. The lighting, fog signal machinery and wireless apparatus were designed by the engineer to the Irish Commissioners. One of the considerations in the design of this vessel was that she had to remain at station in the boisterous weather conditions encountered off the south Irish coast.

The iron and steel *Albatross* built in 1926. This vessel was withdrawn from service in 1970. (Author's Collection)

Her dimensions were, 'length on the waterline, 102 ft., breadth 24 ft 3 inches, depth of hold 12 ft. 6 inches. She was designed to ride a mushroom anchor weighing three and a half tons with 120 to 180 fathoms with no ballast required. The mooring equipment consisted of 440 fathoms in 2 cables of one and three quarter inch open link chain. The vessel also had a spare stretchless anchor weighing 37 cwt.'[60] The main hawse pipes were housed inside steel tubes, allowing them to be easily removed, and they were extended at the lower end well clear of the ships plating by heavy castings designed to prevent chafing of the cable. The anchor cable was operated by compressed air and the cable holders were of wrought iron and brass-bushed. A derrick was also fitted together with a hand-winch for working stores. The chain plates were of the highest quality of forged iron and were riveted to the sheer strake of the vessel. The vessel's bottom structure was of iron.

The mizzen mast

The mizzen mast was a steel tube 90 feet in length fitted with day marks. The main mast was also built of steel and the standing rigging was of the best crucible steel wire. On the top of the main mast was a fixed platform, on which were an external gallery and the lantern – 8 feet in diameter with glazing 4 feet 6 inches high. The lantern was reached by a rigid external steel ladder, from the roof of the deck house with a door opening inwards on to the gallery at the side. The light was produced by autoform incandescent mantles 35 mm in diameter on petroleum vapour burners working at a pressure of 60 lb per square inch. The light was reflected by 24-inch silver-on-copper parabolic reflectors. The power of the beam thrown by each reflector was over 50,000 candles. The reflectors were reused and were over sixty years old, made out of a slab of silver burned on a slab of copper rolled into a plate and hammered into a parabolic form in a mould.

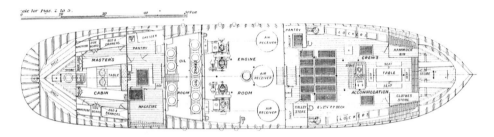

Drawing of the deck of the *Albatross*. Note the crew's accommodation in the fo'c'sle, the location of their lockers, bin for their hammocks and clothes. The Master's accommodation is at the stern. (Author's Collection)

Crew accommodation

The *Albatross* was subdivided into six separate compartments by means of five watertight bulkheads and was thought to be virtually unsinkable. All skylights on the weather deck were watertight and all means of entrance to the lower deck or between decks were inside the deck house. The living quarters for the crew were roomy and comfortable, furnished with wardrobes, tables, seats and each cabin was supplied with a stove, but the crew still slept in hammocks. The Master's cabin was finished in polished mahogany. There was also a fully equipped galley and pantry.

One lifeboat and one cutter were placed on boat platforms at either side of the ship. The davits were fitted with the most up-to-date winches and wire rope fall mechanism so that they could be easily handled. 9 tons of fresh water were held under the lower deck and the oil tanks held over 2,000 gallons. The fuel oil used was the same as that used for the light. Oil was pumped to the light into a pair of horizontal cylindrical tanks bolted to the engine room bulkhead sufficient for about 8-hour operations.

A radio beacon was erected to emit simultaneous and identical signals. The aerial of the radio beacon consisted of two four-wire cage aerials on 18-inch diameter ash hoops suspended at the ends of two 12-foot spreaders from the top of the foremast 31 feet above the sea. In 1955 a new vessel, also named the *Albatross*, was introduced temporarily to replace the Blackwater lightship *Fulmar*. The *Fulmar* had been damaged the previous year when blown from

The galley on the lightship *Guillemot*.
(Jack O'Leary)

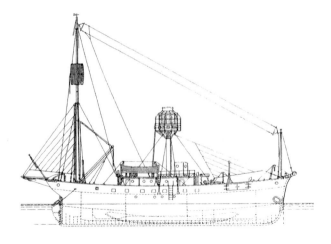

Drawing showing the
electrical radio aerials
on the *Albatross*. Note
the fixed lantern and
the barrel day marker.
(Author's Collection)

her station in severe weather. The second *Albatross*, unlike the old vessels, was
painted red to be more recognisable and was equipped with a more powerful
beacon light that could be seen many miles away. She also had refrigeration and
more advanced cooking facilities. She was replaced with the repaired *Fulmar*
some months later.

Iron and steel: the *Spurn* lightship and the Humber Harbour Board 1927

The *Spurn* lightship was an example of a small iron and steel vessel built in
1927 for the Humber Harbour Board by the Goole Shipbuilding and Repairing
Company Limited at a cost of £17,000. She also had greatly improved
accommodation for crew. In November 1927 she was placed on her station at
the Spurn. This station was at the entrance to the Humber, 4 miles from the
Spurn lighthouse. The vessel was towed into position and moored by means
of a 26 cwt mushroom anchor, with two spare anchors of 9 cwt and 7 cwt
respectively available in case of emergency. At the time it was commented on
how modern a ship she was. She was one of the five lightships on the River
Humber: the *Spurn*, the *Lower Whitton*, the *Middle Whitton*, the *Upper
Whitton* and the *Bull*.

The lantern

The *Spurn* was built of steel and divided into numerous watertight compartments
by seven transverse watertight bulkheads, two longitudinal watertight bulkheads
and eight short transverse watertight bulkheads connecting the longitudinal
bulkheads to the shell. Like the *Albatross* she was believed to be practically

The *Spurn* lightship, built in 1927 for the Humber Harbour Board. (Ewan Monro)

unsinkable. The lantern, with its impressive optical apparatus was supported 35 feet above the waterline by a hollow steel mast, 4 feet in diameter, which contained a vertical ladder for access to the light. She also had two wooden masts to carry the wireless aerial 53 feet above the deck. The light had a power of 18,000 candles and its group flash, white, was visible for 11 miles. Acetylene gas was used for the light and a twelve months' supply could be stored aboard. The optic was mounted on a constant level table controlled by a balance weight which ensured that the table and light remained horizontal, whatever the weather. The light was revolved by a falling weight contained in the mast which still had to be regularly rewound by the crew on watch.[61]

The deck house on the upper deck housed the entrance to the lantern mast, engine room, gas store and the wireless room. The steering gear at the stern of the vessel was used to guide the lightship when she was being towed to and from station. The steering wheel was linked directly to the rudder. There was only a single lifeboat on small vessels like the *Spurn*, but on larger vessels there were two lifeboats, clinker built with airtight compartments.

Wireless

This vessel was equipped with wireless and three types of fog signal, which operated in conjunction with each other, an electric foghorn, a wireless signal and a submarine signal. Ships could thus ascertain their distance and bearings from the lightship, and by means of the wireless the vessel could communicate with other stations. The main fog signal was an electric nautophone, the trumpets of which were fixed at the top of the mast immediately below the lantern giving a blast of two notes every 20 seconds. The wireless fog signal was in Morse Code with a range of 50 miles. Finally, the signal was given by an electric submarine oscillator suspended over the starboard side of the ship which had a maximum range of 20 miles. The vessel had a large capacity storage battery so that all fog signals could be commenced without waiting to start the engine and electric machine.

The crew

The crew of the *Spurn* originally consisted of the Master (or Mate), four seamen, one wireless operator and one engine man. Later the crew was reduced to a total of five. In '1953 wages were £8 16s 0d per week for a Master and £6 14s 7d for a seaman plus uniform. They had risen to £12 12s 9d and £9 19s 6d respectively plus £2 lightship duty allowance and uniforms by 1962.'

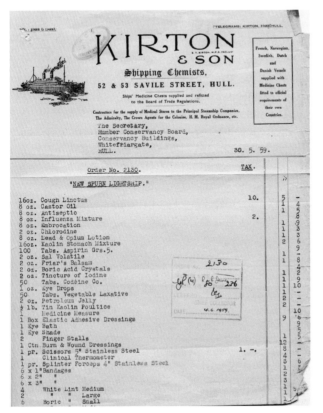

The Master of a lightship was responsible for first aid and the oversight of a basic medicine chest on board. Note the list of first aid and general medicine ordered for the *Spurn* lightship in 1959. (Author)

CHAPTER 9

Lightships in Wartime

Bullets had even penetrated both sides of the thick iron davits. There were at least a dozen bullet holes in the skylight of the Master's cabin.

Lightships during the First World War

Up to the beginning of the First World War, Trinity House was responsible for ninety-six lighthouses and fifty-one lightships. A number of them were withdrawn from service so as not to aid the enemy, but some stayed on station with their lights extinguished and their names painted over; others were illuminated on appropriate occasions to allow for the safe passage of convoys. Trinity House sent out an order to the four vessels on the Goodwin Sands in 1915 instructing them to note enemy aircraft passing within sight of the lookout. All this information was to be noted in the 'log' and sent ashore with the next relief and would have been useless by the time it reached the authorities.[62] Lightship men were paid for reporting the presence of German submarines in their locality. On 16 March 1915 a senior lamplighter, L. Smith, on board the *South Rock* lightship reported a submarine and was awarded £5 11s 7d for his trouble. The rest of the crew also received a payment.

On 21 June 1916, the *Corton* lightship stationed several miles off Yarmouth was sunk by a mine. Five of the crew were killed and the two severely injured were taken to Yarmouth. Captain Rudd was at the bow of the vessel when he sighted the mine and warned his crew. However, the mine was sighted too late and the explosion was so great that the vessel was lifted out of the water, broke up and sank immediately. The two survivors were picked up by a passing fishing boat but there was no sign of the rest of the crew. In early 1915 the Trinity House tender *Irene* was sunk by enemy action with the loss of twenty-eight lives. Later, the Trinity House tender *Alert* was sunk when her anchor fouled a mine, with the loss of eleven lives in April 1917.

Experience of service between the wars

One lightship man spoke of his experience, between the wars, of preparing for his first tour of duty on a lightship. On appointment he,

> had been issued with a hammock, tea pot, enamel mug, plate, and deep dish. The day before I had ordered my stores; tinned milk, fruit, beans, and meat, flour, yeast, jam, butter, lard, eggs, bacon, cheese, potatoes, onions, carrots, peas, and meat, both fresh and salt; in fact enough food for two months. My sea kit, too, was put aboard. It consisted of two canvas bags containing oilskin, jerseys, sea boots, dungarees, lammy coat complete with hood, sea boots stockings, mittens, mufflers, balaclava helmets and of course bedding, blankets and pillows; and finally, a small case containing shore clothes, toilet gear, writing material, a couple of books and a few personal trifles.[63]

Lightship men had always provided their own food and this practice continued until the last manned lightship.[64] The *English and Welsh Grounds* was the oldest vessel operated by Trinity House, built in 1903 by John Crown & Sons, Sunderland. Although the vessel had generators for lighting the lantern she used the original paraffin lamp (9-2 watt oil lamps), which was rotated by a large clockwork motor. This had to be wound up every 30 minutes with a big crank handle.

Heating on board was by coal fires and cooking was done on a coal range, which also provided hot water; fresh water had to be hand-pumped into a header tank for this purpose.

> We did 4 weeks on and 4 weeks off, and had to provide our own food. The pay was not very good but with half our time spent 'at sea' it was adequate. I spent a Christmas on board which I was not looking forward to but it turned out to be quite a special day. It started off like any other day until at 10 a.m. a motor cruiser from Devon came alongside with beer, spirits, mince pies, Christmas puddings, turkey in fact everything for a grand feast. Soon after Barry Lifeboat came alongside with more booze and food but what touched me most was the gifts they brought from school children in Cardiff, mine was a handmade, beautifully embroidered writing case made by a 13 year old girl. I still have it, sadly I lost her details so was never able to write and thank her. Alcohol was not allowed on board but the skipper turned a blind eye although did keep a check on our consumption and made sure we were fit for our duties. Provision of fresh food had always caused problems for lightship men.[65]

Out of a wage of about £12 per month, the lightship man had to purchase enough appropriate food to last for up to two months afloat. Later, food was provided every month. The crew had to keep their food such as meat in an ordinary meat safe. Bread became contaminated by weevils and mould. Meat usually had to be eaten within a few days of coming aboard. Butter and fat soon became rancid.

Arriving on board for the first time between the two world wars

When arriving at his station for the first time the new lightship man climbed a narrow companion way to the crew's quarters, which was rank with the smoke of many varied brands of tobacco and the 'peculiar smell of all ship's fo'c'sle'. He was greeted by friendly faces who no doubt gave him pointers as to how to survive on board for his duration. On starting their two-month tour on station, many would think about the prospect of having left family and friends and ponder on the sameness of everyday life in a tiny isolated vessel in the company of six or seven other men who did not always prove congenial company. However, lightship men worked without a grumble about their conditions but not without grumbling about each other. Going about duties quietly was an absolute must on such a small vessel. It took some time to acquire this ability, as many found out. After his watch, one new crewman went below and used his coffee pot, which had bubbled away during the night. Next morning, when coming off watch, he was accosted with several inquiries as to the noise of his coffee machine 'whom the bloody motor boat belonged'. Another member of the crew peered at him and reprimanded him for sniffing while in his hammock: 'Must you sniff? Ain't yer got a handkerchief?'[66]

Boring chores

Life on a lightship meant that many boring chores had to be carried out on a regular basis. The lightship's boat had to be lowered on calm days to scrub round the waterline to get rid of weed or to touch up the large white letters on the side. The light had to be maintained and cleaned every day, and sometimes seamen had to carry out lamplighters' duties – a difficult and dangerous job – when the individual needed to keep all his wits about him. One slip and he would be seriously or fatally injured. When aloft lighting the lantern, the mast would reel dizzily, the lamplighter or seaman would have to brace themselves on the steel deck of the lantern to adjust the flame of each separate burner. When climbing down the mast from the lantern, the force of the wind would try and pull the crew member from the rigging.

One crewman remembers when he had to fill in for the lamplighter who was ashore,

It was a roughish day, and I climbed in easily to the lantern to light up. Having squirmed into the lantern via a tiny steel door, I turned on the oil, lit the inner and outer wicks and seeing them burning, went below to drop the driving rod which connects the lantern to the mechanism. However on going out on deck, I saw one of the lamps was flaring up and smoking, so I clambered up again. As I stood on

Rope-making on the *Gull* in the 1900s. Rope-making and mat-making were common pastimes among lightship men. (Author's Collection)

the greasy iron plating of the lantern, my feet slipped from beneath me and I fell forward jamming my right eye into one of the very hot smoke stacks. The agony was terrific, to say nothing of the fact that I thought I must have destroyed the sight of one eye. I yelled and at last fell clear.[67]

He was not in this case seriously injured, but many a crewman was seriously and fatally injured when carrying out duties on a vessel in bad weather.

In heavy winter, weather matters could get very much worse. At times large slabs of snow obscured the light and had to be removed. Sometimes this happened so often that the crew took turns to climb, desperately clinging to the ladder, to the lantern to clear it. Down below in the mess, kettles would be chocked off on the stove with 'fiddles' to prevent them being thrown off during the movements of the vessel. Lamps would be lashed to the table.

Spare time was spent fishing or making toys, rope mats or ships in a bottle. To supplement their diet almost every member of the crew made their own bread, for after a short while the fresh bread taken aboard on relief day would go stale and become coated with mould.

The Second World War

At the outbreak of the Second World War, approximately fifty lightships were stationed about the coast of the United Kingdom. Crews worked under different regulations than during peace time as special rules operated during the

1939–1945 period. The men of the service did not see themselves as combatants and some members of Trinity House service resigned as soon as a gun was placed on their vessel. A number of vessels were also withdrawn from service so as not to aid the German fleet. Among those withdrawn were the *Outer Dowsing, Inner Dowsing, Dudgeon, Lynn Well, Smith's Knoll* and *Cromer Knoll*. Some were also withdrawn in the Thames estuary while on the west coast the *St Govan* and those in Morecambe Bay were similarly withdrawn. Buoys had their mooring slipped and were allowed to float out of position or were towed to safe areas.

Trinity House classified lightships as: to be extinguished; to be left burning in the interests of shipping having been dimmed or screened; or to be extinguished except in certain circumstances. A number of vessels were left on station with their names painted out and lights extinguished. These included the *Middle Spurn* lightship, which only gave out a light during certain agreed times. The *Spurn* lightship was moved to the middle Humber position, marking the boom across the river. She was returned in May 1946 to approximately her pre-war position off the entrance to the Humber, where she remained until being withdrawn from station for refitting in 1959. The *North Carr* lightship was moved to a station between the Mull of Kintyre and the Mull of Galloway to mark the entrance to the Clyde. Others who had their lights extinguished were the *Cockle, Newarp, Tongue, Gull, Corton* and *Kentish Knock*. The *Sunk, Cork* and *Tongue* were illuminated during periods to guide convoys in the vicinity. All those on stations unlit remained manned, carrying out surveillance duties, watching mines and sinking them with rifle fire when possible. Many of the Irish lightships were also withdrawn during this period.

The *Sevenstones* lightship was replaced with a lighted buoy during the Second World War. This photograph is of the lightship on this station fully automated and powered by solar energy in the 1980s. (Author's Collection)

Lightships attacked

A number of lightships were attacked by enemy action during the Second World War, and a few on more than one occasion. The Germans suspected lightship crews of observing and reporting German shipping movements. In February 1940, the Transport and General Workers' Union demanded the most complete and effective protection possible for their members employed by Trinity House on lightships and tender service. This protection was requested after the union had received reports of 'cruel and dastardly attacks on these unprotected men'. They asked that both Ernest Bevin, the First Lord of the Admiralty, and the Elder Brethren of Trinity House should provide these ships with the 'proper means of defending themselves'.[68] The *Gull* vessel was attacked in 1941 and was laid up for the duration of the war. *LV80* on the Seven Stones station was frequently bombed and machine gunned by German planes and was replaced by a lighted buoy because of the danger to her crew.

The first lightship attacked by German aircraft was the *Smith's Knoll* on 11 January 1940, and a few months later on 1 November the *LV60* on the *East Ouse* was sunk with six crew members killed. The *Cromer Knoll* and the *Nore* were attacked in 1940 by a German fighter but the *Nore* must have been armed because it was reported that she drove off the attack. On 29 January 1940 the *East Dudgeon*, *LV61*, was bombed and machine-gunned by a Junkers 88 and seriously damaged. The crew of eight took to the boats to save themselves and tried to row to the Wash on the Lincolnshire coast, 25 miles away. In the worst winter weather for over fifty years they capsized close to shore and all were lost except one member of the crew John Sanders. Sanders later told the newspapers, 'We were not alarmed because on previous occasions German pilots had waved to us and left us alone. But, on this occasion the bomber dived suddenly and sprayed the deck with machine-bullets and later dropped nine bombs which hit upon the ship. The ship heeled over and seemed to go right under. The decks were awash and we were floundering about in water.'[69] The Germans later claimed that the lightship was a naval patrol vessel.

The South Folkestone *Gate* was attacked in 1940 and sunk when six aircraft attacked the vessel when the crew were at dinner. Some of the crew managed to escape in the only boat not destroyed before the vessel sank. The Master was

The second *Sevenstones* lightship was attacked and bombed on a number of occasions during the Second World War. (Author's Collection)

In 1940 this vessel, *LV38*, was damaged by the Italian steamer *Erani*. The crew abandoned the lightship and reached safety. *LV38* served on the Gull station and was transferred to the Mouse station in 1940. (Author's Collection)

THV *Reculver* was badly damaged in 1940. Fifty-five men were wounded and one officer killed. She was repaired but was again attacked again by German aircraft later that year. (Author's Collection)

injured and two of the crew killed. After visiting the *East Dudgeon* lightship in 1944, which had been damaged, one writer commented:

> I had examined the S-Lightship. She was worse than a colander. The lantern was smashed, her sides pierced by cannon shell and armour-piercing bullets, the life boats shot into a mere boat-shaped mess of splinters, hanging from the davits ... Bullets had even penetrated both sides of the thick iron davits. There were at least a dozen bullet holes in the skylight, on the Master's cabin.[70]

The same writer later observed Stukas dive-bombing the old *East Sand Head* lightship, which at the time was unmanned. In all, twenty-seven lightship men of Trinity House were killed in the Second World War and twenty lightships lost to enemy action.

When these men came ashore they still had some difficult situations to experience. Sometimes they had to leave the lightship at very short notice because of the danger of attack. Writing of his experience when taken ashore, George Goldsmith Carter recalled the bitter inhospitable treatment he met at the hands of the caretaker of the Trinity House Pilot depot: 'It was the only place available to us. Yet as we were light vessel ratings, and not pilots, we were told to dump our belongings on the side walk. On no account could we take them in, as he knew nothing about us and had not been informed of our coming. The caretaker graciously permitted us to shelter in a cellar beneath the offices.'[71]

Lightships were not the only Trinity House vessels damaged by enemy aircraft, indeed relief tenders of Trinity House and the Commissioners of Irish Lights were also targeted. The Trinity House tender *Reculver* was attacked on 9 January 1940 just after supplying stores to the *Cockle* lightship. Some of the crew relieved from the *Cockle* were among the fifty or so injured in the incident, with one fatality. The *Reculver* was disabled by the attack but was towed into Yarmouth by the *Patricia*, another tender. The *Reculver* was repaired but later struck a mine in October of that year – five crew members were injured, and she sank.

D-Day landings

During the D-Day landings a large number of ships operated in the landing area. Juno Beach was marked with a lightship to aid in the safe navigation of shipping traffic. *LV72 Juno*, was built in 1903 and she saw service in a variety of different stations until the Second World War. During the landings in Normandy she marked a safe passage through a minefield for the landing craft on route to the invasion beaches from June 1944 until January 1945. She was damaged on station in a collision in heavy seas and towed to Le Havre for repairs. After repairs she was placed at a station named the Seine. In March 1946, she was replaced by a French lightship. After the war this vessel later saw service at Smith Knoll station, the Varne station and at other stations until 1954 when she was retired from service. In 1972 she was laid up in Swansea and later sold to the Steel Supply Company in Neath for scrap the following year.

The lightship *LV72 Juno* as a wreck near Neath Abbey, Swansea. Built in 1903 using the same hull plate and rivet construction made famous by the *Titanic*. She marked a safe passage through a minefield for the landing craft on route to the invasion beaches. She was withdrawn from service in 1972 and is the only iron lightship still in existence. (Ben Salter)

CHAPTER 10
English Lightship Tragedies and Heroes

Suddenly saw the liner loom up at me in front of us like a huge ghost, and, of course it was only a matter of seconds before we were in the water.

Danger on the lightships

Danger on lightships was a constant companion as the anchored vessel could do little to escape the behaviours of incompetent skippers or ships swept onto sandbanks or rocks. Many members of the lightship community agree that, given a quiet or busy station, they would prefer the danger of a busy station. Not that they welcomed danger, but a busy station broke the monotony of the daily routine. Life was certainly more interesting in crowded waters, but in busy waters there was a much greater chance of getting into trouble or being run down in dense fog. The Humber estuary, for example, was a very busy area and the lightships stationed there were on many occasions damaged or run down by

Lightship on the Goodwin Sands in bad weather. The lanterns are lowered into the cast iron housing on the deck so that they can be cleaned by the lamplighter. (Author's Collection)

passing ships, usually in dense fog. A number of other stations about the British Isles and Irish coast were particularly dangerous, such as those on the Goodwin Sands, Kish Bank, Daunt Rock and the coast of Scotland. Between 1894 and 1929 at least fourteen Trinity House lightships were sunk in collisions.

The *Sevenstones* lightship 1841

The Seven Stones reef has been a navigational hazard to shipping for hundreds of years. The rocks are only exposed at half-tide and it was never feasible to build a lighthouse on the site. Many wrecks are recorded, including the infamous oil tanker the *Torrey Canyon*, which sank in 1967. In 1826 an unsuccessful petition was sent to Parliament to position a lighthouse on the reef, followed by a second petition in 1839 by merchants from Liverpool and the Bristol Channel. Trinity House had sent a survey team to take soundings of the Seven Stones and proposed a lightship instead. A lightship was eventually provided and moored off the Seven Stones Reef, nearly 15 miles to the west-north-west of Land's End, Cornwall, and 7 miles east-north-east of the Isles of Scilly. The first lightship was moored near the reef in 1841 in over 40 fathoms. She was built of wood, with a tonnage of 162, her length was 80 feet, breadth 21 feet, and her two masts for the lights were 69-feet and 60-feet tall. Red balls were fixed on each mast to distinguish her from other light vessels. Two lights displayed at 38 feet, and 20 feet were of the catoptric system and could be seen from 10 miles away. She also carried a gong fog signal. By 1891, only one light was displayed at 38 feet with three quick flashes followed by 36 seconds of darkness. Originally, there was a crew of ten with five on station at a time.

The weather and tides on the Seven Stones station could be tricky, and within three days of being placed on station, in August 1841, she had dragged her anchor in bad weather and was out of position for a time. She was placed back on station after four days and a few months later she again drifted from her anchorage and, as a result, she was provided with a new mushroom anchor. In November 1842 her cable parted and she was almost wrecked when she drove over the reef at high tide. As she carried one lugsail, a staysail and a jib, the crew were able to steer her to New Grimsby from where she was towed back to her station, but the following January she broke adrift again. Two months later, in March, she was again found drifting in a moderate south-westerly breeze, and was once again towed to New Grimsby and then taken back to her position a few days later.

Despite this station experiencing severe weather on a regular basis, the lightships usually held firm and the Lighthouse Commissioners later reported in 1859 on the crew: 'The men, eleven, were clean and neatly dressed; the vessel very clean and newly painted. The shape of the vessel appears slightly sharper

The *Sevenstones* lightship was hit by a meteorite on a night in November 1872. (Author's Collection)

forward than that of the others visited. She is eighteen years old and is provided with guns and a gong.'[72] The Master of the lightship thought that, because of the length of the sea, she rode better than vessels in a shorter sea.

The Island of Tresco was thought the most convenient place to accommodate the crew as the lightship could be seen from there and it was also a safe harbour. Provisions were procured by crews themselves rowing and sailing to New Grimsby in the lightship's longboat. In October 1851, one of the longboats capsized in bad weather while they were on their way back from Scilly with stores, all the crew were lost. Augustus Smith, the Governor of the Isles of Scilly, later had an acrimonious disagreement with Trinity House about crew accommodation and, after some correspondence in 1868, accommodation for the crew and provisions were provided instead at Penzance.[73]

A night in November 1872 would have been a memorable one for the crew when a meteor exploded over the ship, showering the deck with cinders. It was reported to the Royal Society, London, 'that the watch were struck senseless for a short period, seeing nothing before the shock, but that, on recovery, balls of fire like large stars were falling in the water like splendid fireworks, and the decks were covered with cinders, which crushed under the sailors feet as they walked'. The crew reported a smell of brimstone and that all the cinders were later washed off the ship by daybreak.[74]

In January 1873 the barque *Athole* came too close to the vessel and fouled the lightship's rigging and starboard light. She was again severely damaged in gales in October 1886 when she took on water. On 29 December 1900 she suffered severe storm damage when a large section of her bulwarks were carried away and one of her boats wrecked. During this episode two members of the crew were injured, one of them seriously. In 1908 one member of the crew fell off the main deckhouse and died as a result of a broken neck. All of these incidents took place before the introduction of wireless and it would have taken a long time for help to arrive. Contact with the shore was dependent on passing vessels being willing to bring news to a nearby port.[75]

A new vessel took up position on the Sevenstones during the Second World War, which was later replaced with a lighted buoy after being frequently bombed and machine-gunned by German pilots. After the war the buoy was replaced with a lightship that later broke adrift in March 1948 and ended up on Pendeen Watch on the north Cornish coast. In 1954 she undertook a refit with the provision of hot water, electric lighting, refrigerator, one- and two-berth cabins and a roomy mess deck. Daily work on the ship such as watch-keeping and maintenance of the 600,000-candlepower lantern could be carried out without going outside. Previously the refit crew had to climb up the mast every morning to trim the lamps, hauling their supply of oil with them; a dangerous task in rough weather. By 1987 the *Sevenstones* lightship had been automated and she now also acts as an automatic weather station.

The *Newarp* lightship 1884

On occasions lightships have been run down, damaged or sunk. Surprisingly, in view of the code of the sea that all should help other vessels in trouble, offending vessels have sometimes sailed or steamed away without reporting the incident or trying to help the lightship crew. Such a case was the incident of the *Newarp* lightship and the sailing ship *Star of the Sea* in April 1884.

The *Star of the Sea* was a small schooner, built in 1856, registered in Ipswich, of 111 tons. She had left Harwich on 26 April with a crew of five hands. Later that day she arrived off Lowestoft and at about midnight an ordinary seaman named Southgate was at the wheel supported by an able seaman on watch. The Master ordered that the vessel's course be altered, intending to pass the lightship to windward but finding that the tide was changing the course was altered, bringing the lightship on the schooner's port bow. This manoeuvre would have taken him leeward of the lightship safely. However, these instructions were not supported by the men on watch or any of the witnesses who stated that the lightship was on the schooners starboard bow. Some 5 or 10 minutes before the

The *Newarp* lightship was hit by a passing ship that did not stop to offer assistance. This wooden vessel was built in 1869 and decommissioned in 1945. *LV68*, which served on the Seven Stones station, also served on the Kansas station during the Normandy landings with *Juno* during the Second World War. (Author's Collection)

collision, the Master of the *Star of the Sea* had gone below. The lookout watch, seeing that she was bearing down on the lightship, tried to help the helmsman but, despite their efforts, the schooner hit the lightship amidships on the port side. The lightship lost some of her stanchions and bulwarks and some of her main rigging and suffered other damage. As soon as the schooner cleared the lightship, she continued on her course and, not being able to reach her original destination, put into Sunderland.

The board of enquiry found that the Master was to blame for the collision. As well as having run away from the lightship, he later endeavoured to conceal the fact that he had been in a collision. Surprisingly the enquiry found that they had no power to punish the Master as he did not have a relevant Master's certificate that they could deal with. The Master therefore escaped any punishment.

The sinking of the *Girdlar* lightship 1884

About midnight on Friday 20 June 1884, the *Girdlar*, a wooden lightship, was run down by the Peninsular & Oriental Steamer *Indus*, a vessel of 2,000 tons. The *Indus* had left the Thames proceeding to Sidney with over 400 passengers on board and all went well until the vessel ran into the lightship in the Prince's Channel. No explanation was ever given for the collision as the *Indus* had a pilot on board. The pilot was unable or perhaps did not want, to give any explanation for the collision. The lightship had taken the usual precautions, lookouts had been kept, and the crew, seeing the large vessel bearing down on them, prepared to abandon the vessel by jumping on board the *Indus* when she was engaged with the lightship. The lightship sank within 3 minutes after the collision. All seven of the lightship crew were saved and brought to Dover. The *Indus* later continued on her journey. The *Girdlar* lightship had another near miss in March 1898 in severe weather when she received serious damage after being driven by a severe northerly gale against Margate pier. The *Quiver* lifeboat was launched and with difficulty extricated her from that position and towed her into the harbour. Four of the horses used to launch the lifeboat were drowned during the operation.

The *Morecambe Bay* lightship: run down on 16 July 1903

In 1903 the *Morecambe* lightship, a new vessel which had cost over £20,000, was run down in the early morning fog by a passing coaster, the *Abbot*. This new vessel had only been on her station for ten weeks before the collision occurred. The lightship had a crew of seven hands and one engineer, who was on board for the purpose of instructing the crew in the use of the new fog

The *Morecambe Bay* lightship was sunk in 1903. She was first placed on station in 1863 and showed a red revolving light. The vessel illustrated was later placed on this station. (Author's Collection)

signals. The *Abbot* was observed by the watch on the lightship and when she was about 300 yards from the lightship and heading south-east it was observed that there was no person on deck on watch. The lightship hailed the *Abbot* and got no reply. They then saw a man stumbling up on the port side toward the wheel but it was too late to prevent the collision. At about 6.35 a.m. the *Abbot* struck the lightship with her stern nearly at right angles under the port bow. The watertight bulkhead of the lightship kept her afloat for 15 minutes, allowing the crew to launch a boat and get aboard the coaster. The lightship later sank with no loss of life. The crew who had been picked up by the *Abbot* were taken into nearby Fleetwood.

When giving evidence to the Board of Inquiry one of the crew of the *Abbot* stated that, as they were passing the lightship, they saw a member of the crew waving at them. Thinking that the lightship wanted to pass letters on for posting, he steered for the lightship without orders from his captain. The lightship crew denied that they had hailed the *Abbot* or signalled her until they had seen her sailing directly for the lightship and a collision was imminent. The court found that the captain of the *Abbott* was not justified in leaving the bridge in charge of an able seaman and that he had not sufficiently instructed him before going below. The watch had not been appropriate for the safe navigation of the vessel. It was agreed that a good and proper lookout had not been kept and the collision and loss of the lightship was caused by the wrongful act and default of the Master of the *Abbott*. No blame was attached to the Master of the lightship, Thomas Williams.

The sinking of the *Gull* lightship March 1929 and the loss of the Master

Of all the 'signposts' of the sea one of the best known was the *Gull* which lay on the Gull Stream, one of the busiest shipping highways in the world. The *Gull* is believed to have first gone on station in 1860 at Lynn Well where it remained until 1928 when it was transferred to the Gull station on the Goodwin Sands. Lightships bear the names of the places where they are stationed, so she became known as the *Gull* during her tour of duty there. The *Gull* marked the channel between the Brake Sand and the west side of the Goodwins. She was believed to be the second oldest lightship in European waters. Built in 1860, and named the *Downe*, her overall length was 90 feet, maximum breadth 21½ feet, depth below upper deck 11 feet and she weighed 189 tons. She exhibited a revolving white light at 38 feet above sea level that flashed four times every 20 seconds. This light was visible for over 7 miles and she was marked with the name *Gull* in large white letters on a red painted hull. She was manned by a Master or Mate and six seamen with two men keeping watch at all times.

The *Gull* was continuously threatened by the careless navigation of passing ships but never under such tragic circumstances as on 18 March 1929 when, in thick fog, she was hit by the *City of York*. The lightship was severely damaged on the port side just aft of 'midships' near the Master's cabin and sank in over 7 fathoms of water. The crew were rescued by the *City of York* but the Master, Captain Williams, drowned. One of the crew of the *Gull*, Mr Good, who was on watch, told his story of the disaster to a local newspaper. The first he knew of any danger was when he 'suddenly saw the liner loom up at me in front of us like a huge ghost, and, of course it was only a matter of seconds before we were in the water. Fortunately I was able to hang on to one of the boats, which I cut loose, and rowed about looking for the other men … Luckily the sea was calm.' Mr Good was able to pick up some of the crew. Mr Richmond, a lamp attendant, was in his bunk when the collision occurred at about 3.30 a.m. He had heard a loud crash and in less than a minute found himself in the water being picked up his colleague, Mr Good. 'Richmond said it was pitch black,' and 'very eerie' when the liner hit the lightship. All he could hear was 'the hooting of the sirens and the shouting of a man,' which was Mr Good in one of the boats.[76] The liner was so big that the passengers did not become aware

The *Gull* lightship as a wreck. *LV38* was built in 1866 constructed of teak on an oak frame. Her hull was copper sheeted. She took at least ten years to complete as the teak and oak had to mature. The ship sank in 1929 after a collision with the liner *City of York*. Raised and repaired, it continued on the Brake station until it suffered another collision in 1940. In 1946 it was sold to the Thurrock Yacht Club at Grays. (Author's Collection)

of the collision at the time. The damage to the lightship was so extensive that she sank almost immediately and the crew were thrown into the cold water. The lightship had almost been cut in two.

The *Lady Beatty*, the local lifeboat from Deal, was immediately launched. The fog was the worst experienced in the channel that winter, so the lifeboat had to be steered by compass. It reached the sunken lightship when the visibility was 'about half a dozen yards'. When the lifeboat reached the lightship all that could be seen was the top of the lightship mast a little above the waves. After towing some wreckage to Deal, the lifeboat was sent back to the Gull station to act as a temporary light. The lifeboat had been placed in a very dangerous position using only an old hand-held foghorn and a bell to warn passing vessels of the danger of the sunken lightship and treacherous sands. The Coxswain of the lifeboat had managed to obtain an old fog signal apparatus, some flares and a large ship's bell. He told a local newspaper, 'We then stood by, eyes, and ears alert for very real danger, which threatened us on all sides. Around us were ships groping their way through the fog sounding their foghorns, and the noise of their propellers as they churned up the water was even louder'. Several times the lifeboat had to move out of the path of oncoming vessels. Later, when the fog lifted, on, 'three distinct occasions our shouting and waving recalled three vessels who were heading straight for the treacherous sandbank. Had we not been there these ships would have all stranded in another minute or so.'[77]

The *Lady Beatty* was eventually relieved by the Trinity House steamer *Satellite* after a short period. A week later, the nearby *North Goodwin* lightship just managed to prevent by warning blasts the steamer *Coniscrag* from colliding with it. The weather was exceedingly foggy at the time and the steamer was unaware of the lightship until she heard the siren blasts. The *Gull* was salvaged in July and beached at Deal, from where it was towed to Ramsgate. It was made

LV81, the *North Goodwin* lightship. This vessel was the first all-electric lightship for Trinity House. (Author's Collection)

seaworthy before being taken to North Shields in tow of the tug *Cullercoats* for a complete refit. The vessel then returned to the Goodwin Sands station, which by this time was located closer to Brake Sands and known as the Brake station. The vessel was renamed the *Brake* accordingly.

The *Brake* lightship: holed in an incident in 1940

On 16 January 1940, the lightship on the Brake station was hit by the *Ernani*, an Italian steamer. In very bad weather, a north-east gale and blizzard, the *Brake* was holed in the collision but the crew of twelve were saved. The *Ernani* had been anchored nearby waiting for clearance to enter harbour but she began to drag her anchor in the terrible weather conditions and hit the *Brake*, holing her below the waterline. The Master of the *Brake* became concerned as he thought that she might founder and he gave the order to abandon ship. The weather was too rough to allow the *Ernani* to take the lightship crew on board, so they rowed on for 1 hour until they were picked up by HMS *Holdfast*. The lightship, however, remained afloat and some of the crew returned to her early next morning. She was later towed stern first to Harwich for repair. When repaired she was placed on the Mouse station near Maplin sands in the Thames estuary, where she was attacked in 1941 by the Luftwaffe. She was later replaced and laid up for the remainder of the war.

The *Brake* was built in 1860. Her light was shown from a lantern on a mast amidships. She sank in 1928 after a collision but was repaired and decommissioned in 1946. (Author's Collection)

Lightships on the dangerous Goodwin Sands

The Goodwin Sands lie almost on the threshold of the Port of London. At their longest they are more than 6 miles on the seaward side, and at the widest they are 4½ miles across. The Goodwin Sands have been well-known for centuries as a dangerous place as the sandbanks and channels continually alter position and shape. The sands have been the graveyard to Viking long ships, Saxon ships, galleons, modern liners and even lightships. Shakespeare, in the *Merchant of Venice*, refers to these sands as 'very dangerous flat and fatal, where the carcases of many a tall ship lie buried.' Parts of the sands are uncovered at low tide, and when the weather is fine they can be visited by tourists who play cricket on them. When covered by the tide, they constitute a grave danger to shipping.

The first recorded shipwreck on the Goodwin Sands dates to 1298. The sands would not have earned their terrible reputation had they not lain in the path of the busiest shipping route in the world. As they are some 5 miles off the Kent coast, they are directly in the route of all shipping traffic bound to and from the Thames or the North Sea and the English Channel. The greatest loss of life on the sands was in 1703 as a result of the Great Storm, when many vessels, including large war ships, had to take refuge in the downs to ride out the storm. Thirteen Man'o' War were lost and over 2,000 crew. There have also been other notable wrecks since that date. Ships that became stranded on the sands faced a terrible fate – the sands could break their backs as the tide changed. Survivors may have been able to clamber onto the sands as the tide receded, light fires and attempt to attract the attention of people on the nearby coast, but within hours

The first safety beacon erected on the Goodwin Sands in 1840. This structure, made of oak and guyed up by chains, survived two years. Shipwrecked mariners could climb the ladder, if they could get to the beacon, take refuge in the 'top' and raise a blue flag to signal the Deal boatmen to put to sea and, hopefully, effect a rescue. (Author's Collection)

the tide would return. If no help was forthcoming, then the sands would turn into lethal quicksand, and ships and survivors would be engulfed.

Lightships were used sometimes as a place of refuge for shipwrecked mariners. Many sailors on vessels wrecked on the sands were thankful for the efforts of lightship crews who came to their rescue. The *Brake* lightship, because of her position, was called on a number of times to offer refuge to men whose ships had sunk in fog. These lightships were positioned to warn not only passing shipping of danger, but also to alert the local lifeboats when a ship became stranded.

The first lightship on the sands

Since the early 1700s the sands were marked by unlit buoys and later by lightships. In fog or poor visibility, the lightships sounded a powerful diaphone, or hooter, each lightship on the sands giving a different number of blasts so passing vessels could recognise what part of the sands they were approaching and could lay a course away from the danger. The first lightship positioned on the Goodwins was at North Sand Head in 1795. This vessel was an old wooden hulk, lit with nothing more powerful than four tallow candles on a cross piece of wood. In 1809, a second lightship was positioned on the western edge of the Goodwin's in the Gull stream. The name 'Gull' is derived from the French 'guile', the mouth of a channel or stream. The *Gull* had a mast and yard from each end of which hung lanterns. The final two lightships were added at South Sand Head in 1832. All these early vessels were primitive and unreliable, and their lights feeble and mooring not too sound. In bad weather or fog, all the crew could do was anxiously watch their cable, praying it would not brake or that passing ships would not run them down. Lightships were not themselves without tragedy, for example in 1954 the *South Sand* lightship was wrecked and all seven crew lost, the only survivor being a researcher.

The wreck of the *South Goodwin* 1954 and the loss of the crew

The *South Goodwin* lightship was constructed from iron and steel and equipped with four main mushroom-shaped anchors to help stabilise her position. She was stationed in a prominent position about 4 miles off Dover, a position that could be very uncomfortable in bad weather. A lightship had been stationed on this spot called the South Sand Head for some years and a number of them had narrow escapes. In 1899 a vessel on this station broke her moorings in bad weather and went aground. The severe weather prevented the men from being rescued for three days. When the weather later improved, the vessel was towed

The *South Goodwin* lightship. (Author's Collection)

back to her station. In 1914 the *South Goodwin* dragged her anchor and broke from her moorings. She missed going aground on the sands and ended up off Margate with all on board safe.

In 1954 the *South Goodwin*, LV90, which had been built in 1937, was well equipped. All the crew were looking forward to Christmas. A local boat had delivered gifts and food to the crew for the festivities. Gales of exceptional force had been blowing for several days off the east Kent coast and on 26 November 1954 the weather turned increasingly worse, with hurricane winds and massive swells. It was one of the worst storms in the two previous centuries. The lightship simply could not cope with such weather for an extended period of time, and to make matters worse she had only some of her storm anchors in place. The weather was indeed extraordinary, the wind was a force ten to eleven and at about midnight the tide had been running north at its maximum. Huge waves were breaking on the deck and the ship pitched and tossed, putting a great strain on the 410 meters of heavy cable. The moorings were under enormous strain and eventually one of the links broke. Without the security of her anchors, the lightship was at the mercy of the seas.

It was sometime about midnight that the cable parted, but as the vessel was taking such a battering and the motion of the vessel was so violent no one on board would have known she was adrift. Even if the crew had recognised the danger they would have been powerless to do anything. Why no distress signal was sent still remains a mystery, but the wireless aerial may have been seriously damaged in the bad weather. The crew on watch on the nearby *North East Goodwin* lightship saw her sweep past at a fast speed and later saw her hit the sands over 6½ miles north of her usual position. They alerted Trinity House and the coastguards as the *South Goodwin* collapsed onto her starboard side, trapping the seven crewmen inside the ship's hull. Because of the extreme weather, rescuers were unable to reach the stricken lightship.

During a lull in the weather an American helicopter passing over the wreck spotted someone clinging to the rails. Ronald Murton, one member of the crew, had been on board for only a month; aged twenty, Murton was a Ministry of

Agriculture officer who had been observing bird migration. He was rescued after spending 8 hours clinging to the rigging attached to the lantern. He had earlier spent the night in the warm galley wrapped in an old army heavy coat over his pyjamas. Murton had managed to escape from the cabin by pushing up the galley skylight escape hatch. Other members of the crew were unable to follow because of the sea breaking over the vessel. Murton had eventually to abandon any attempt to save his fellow crew members. He later explained that he had heard sounds from the aft end of the deckhouse but he was by then too weak to help. He held out for over 8 hours before he was winched to safety. It was only when the storm had ceased that lifeboats and divers reached the vessel. Not a single body was found and all crew were assumed to be lost at sea. It was thought that the sea had gushed into the cabin space where the crew were sheltering, flooding it.[78] The crew of the stricken lightship had come from the east-coast seafaring counties of Essex, London, Kent, Norfolk and Suffolk.

The East Goodwin adrift 1961

On the night of 12 November 1961, the *East Goodwin* lightship broke adrift and was off station for four days. She had been parted from her mooring in a north-easterly gale. When the crew realised that she was drifting they carried out the appropriate operations to check the drifting. When she was checked she was found to be riding in 130 fathoms, about 6 miles out of position and just 2 miles east of her sister ship the *South Goodwin*. The *Walmer* lifeboat attended the lightship all the night of Sunday 12th. The Trinity House tender, TVH *Vestal*, arrived later that day, after a very rough 9½-hour journey, with a new cable to be placed on board the lightship. The lifeboat stood by the lightship but the weather deteriorated to reach a force-ten gale. The lightship continued to drag a short distance but was still in a secure position. By Tuesday the weather had improved a little to allow the Trinity House steamer to pass a new riding cable, of about 270 fathoms in length, and a 5-ton anchor to the lightship. The work of passing such a heavy cable and anchor was a very difficult and dangerous operation – even in the improving weather the job took all afternoon. It was not until the next day that the weather abated a little so the lightship could be towed back into position. The crew on the lightship had passed a very uncomfortable night in a force-ten gale and very heavy seas waiting for a change so she could be towed back to her station.

The *Varne* almost wrecked in 1966

On the night of 1/2 December 1966, the *Varne* lightship, *LV95*, dragged her anchor under appalling weather conditions and was almost wrecked on nearby shoals.

The *Varn* lightship, now automated. Built in 1958 she served for some time on the Seven Stones station and transferred to the Varne station in 2003. (Mark S.)

The weather was so bad, a south-westerly force-ten gale with a heavy sea and rain, that the Master did not realise that she had drifted off station until he was informed by the coastguard at Folkestone that her bearing had altered. The Master found it difficult to check his position because he could not see his usual marks. During the heavy weather she had been riding about 150 fathoms of cable, which was taut and gave no sign that she was dragging, but the signal from the coastguard indicated that she was about ¾ mile off her station. This signal had also been picked up by the local Trinity House tender that put to sea to tow the vessel back to station. When the tender *Siren* reached the lightship on 2 December she was found to be over 2 miles off station with the weather deteriorating. She was flying the 'Off Station' signals. The lightship held her position at the edge of the shoal, but as the weather deteriorated the tender could not reach her.

The lifeboat at Dover was called out to take the crew off, an action which was accomplished under very dangerous conditions at about midnight on 2 December. During the evacuation the lifeboat sustained serious damage after breaking the glass in one of the lightship's engine room portholes. One lifeboat crewman, a veteran of hundreds of channel rescues, said, 'this was about the most hazardous job we've had'.[79] The lifeboat, because of the damage sustained, was escorted into Dover harbour by the Trinity House tender. The lightship crew were given food and clothing and by the morning of 3 December the weather had improved, which allowed the crew to return to the lightship. She was eventually towed back to her assigned position and resumed her role.

The *Varne LV21* in collision with the *Ore Meteor* 1981

LV21 was built in 1963 and was a 40-meter steel-hulled lightship and one of the last to be commissioned by Trinity House. She saw most of her service off the Kent coast on the Varne, East Goodwin and Channel stations. She was involved in a number of incidents during her long career until she was decommissioned in 2008. The *Varne* is recognised as a ship of national historic importance and has been officially included in the Register of National Historic Ships as No. 2330.

In 1981 she was involved in one of the worst collisions in which any lightship had survived. On Sunday 28 June 1981, about 5.30 p.m, the *Ore Meteor* was being towed to Southampton when she collided with the lightship in a six- to seven-force wind with good visibility but a rough sea. The tug appeared, to those watching on the lightship, as not being powerful enough to tow such a large vessel. The tow and tug passed so close to the lightship that it was in danger of hitting her. The tug attempted to change course by swinging the *Ore Meteor* away from the lightship, but in carrying out this manoeuvre the side of the towed ship hit the *Varne*, causing extensive damage to the upper section of her bow plates. As the lightship drifted back into position, the *Ore Meteor*'s stern equipment fouled the stays of the *Varne*'s foremast. When the *Ore Meteor* pulled away, the lightship foremast was toppled and the lantern demolished with the aft mast of the lightship. However, no damage was done below the waterline. Despite the extensive destruction to the lantern little damage was done to the optics, which the crew proceeded to protect. The whole episode was seen by passengers on the cross-channel ferry. Within a few hours the Trinity House tender, TVH *Siren* arrived and kept the lightship illuminated with searchlights during the night. The lightship was later towed to Southampton for repairs.

The *Spurn* lightship: stationed in the dangerous Humber estuary

The *Spurn* lightship is another example of a vessel placed in a particularly busy and dangerous position. The area is prone to heavy weather, fast tides and fog. Over the years lightships on this station have been hit many times by passing vessels. In January 1930 the *Spurn* lightship was struck and damaged by a fishing trawler and nine years later was hit again and damaged by the SS *Koranton*. The Master of the *Koranton* did not stop to see if the lightship or her crew needed help but carried on his voyage. He also failed to report the collision. It was not until 36 hours later that the agents for the ship reported the incident. The Master was later found guilty by a local court and was 'fined £5 and 4s costs'. In 1938 a Grimsby steam trawler, the *Lord Shewsbury*, collided with the lightship. The Skipper again failed to report the collision and was fined '£10 with £1.15s costs'.

On the Middle station in January 1940, HMT *Adder* struck the lightship and damaged her rigging, wireless cable and shrouds. Two years later she was again damaged in a collision with the HMS *H.42* and had to be dry-docked and repaired. In 1943 she dragged her anchor, was off station for three days and a new mushroom anchor had to be fitted. Four years later, the steamship *Bravo* struck her, which led to her being withdrawn soon after for repairs. She was again struck in 1951 by a passing vessel, a trawler, and her main top mast was damaged, preventing her emitting beacon signals. In 1953 the vessel *Polo* rammed her in a fog and some weeks later in February of that year she lost her moorings and drifted 12 miles. Because of the very bad weather it was a week before she was back on station. In January 1955 and January 1956 she was again damaged by passing vessels.

It was not until some years later that the next serious collision occurred. In October 1962 a vessel, the *Lord Essenden*, collided with the lightship and less than a month later she was again hit by a another passing vessel. The following year in September, and again in November of the following year, she was involved in collisions. In 1963, 1964 and 1965 she also suffered damage. She was extensively damaged in a collision in December 1966 and had to be withdrawn from station as a consequence. The lightship on the Spurn station was finally withdrawn in November 1975.

The lightship *Sula*, decommissioned in 1985, was originally stationed at the mouth of the Humber estuary. (David)

CHAPTER 11

Lightships in Scottish Waters

Given its position the *North Carr* was particularly vulnerable in bad weather.

The Northern Lighthouse Board

The Northern Lighthouse Board is the General Lighthouse Authority for Scotland and the Isle of Man, responsible for marine navigation aids around those coastal areas. It was formed in 1786 as 'The Commissioners of Northern Light Houses', to oversee the construction and operation of four Scottish lighthouses: Kinnaird Head, North Ronaldsay, Scalpay and Mull of Kintyre. Only three manned lightships were ever stationed on the coast of Scotland. The absence of lightships on this coast can be accounted for by the fact that the coast is very rocky and more suitable to the building of lighthouses. A few unmanned lightships were placed in certain positions about the coast, but they did not prove suitable in the long run. The *Otter Rock* lightship was placed on station at a cost of £300 in 1901. She broke her mooring on many occasions, the last time being in January 1958 when she was finally taken off station and scrapped. A second vessel called the *Skeirinoe* was placed in the Little Minch on 26 May 1906 and remained on station until 1963. The third and last unmanned lightship was placed at Cath Sgeir, off the Island of Gigha, in 1905. She was removed at the start of the Second World War and was never replaced.

The first manned lightship the *Pharos*

The first lightship purchased by the Northern Lighthouse Board was an ex-Dutch fishing lugger, flat-bottomed and rounded at the stem and stern. She was used by Robert Stevenson when he was engaged to build the Bell Rock lighthouse. To house the workmen he moored a temporary lightship near the rock. At least forty-eight people lived on the *Pharos*, which included Stevenson

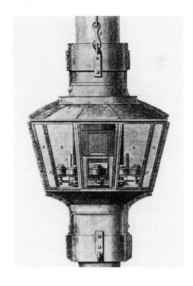

The lantern used on the *Pharos*, designed by
Stephenson in 1807. (Author's Collection)

himself, construction workers and the lightship crew. All were accommodated
in this small craft of just 67 feet long and 16 feet in breadth. In July 1807 she
was overhauled and rigged for her new purpose as a lightship and renamed the
Pharos. She had three masts with a light on each during the hours of darkness
and could be seen 10 miles away.

The light designed by Robert Stevenson himself was visible in all directions.
The lantern was built around the masts so that it could be raised and lowered
for cleaning and lighting. The vessel had three masts. Each mast had a lantern
consisting of a circle of lights with reflectors behind them.

The *Abertay* lightship: the first lightship in Europe to be automated

The second manned lightship in Scottish waters was the *Abertay Spit*, a vessel
anchored in 5½ fathoms. The Arbroath-built *Abertay* was launched on Monday
10 September 1877 and placed on station at the eastern end of Abertay Sands,
off the east coast of Scotland, later that year. She was coloured red. She was for
ten years the only manned lightship in Scottish waters, painted red and had two
masts. Little is known of the history of this vessel.

The second lightship named *Abertay* was built for the Dundee Harbour
Trust and cost £36,000. She was launched on 18 April 1939 and delivered
to the Harbour Trust on 10 July 1939. The light vessel was positioned to
mark the outer limit of the lengthy and dangerous channel into Dundee, near the
extensive Abertay Sands. In May 1945 she was repositioned to mark the end of
an offshore swept channel but she was later stationed in the Tay in early 1946.

The vessel was withdrawn, in June 1953, pending the delivery of essential
equipment. In October of that year the Dundee pilots asked the pilotage

authority when the *Abertay* lightship would be replaced as the buoy that replaced her was inadequate during the winter months in bad weather. In 1971, at a cost of £120,000, she became the first lightship in Europe to be automated and was painted black instead of red. In 1984 she was withdrawn from service and replaced by a high focal plane buoy. She was sold to Trinity House and renamed *LV25* when she was converted to an unmanned lightship.

The *North Carr* lightship – at first only a fog signal vessel

The third and last manned Scottish lightship was stationed at North Carr Rock, situated at the turning point for vessels entering the Forth bound for the Tay. At this point there is a reef of sunken rocks that extends from the shore for over 1½ miles. The rock has been responsible for numerous casualties and loss of life, especially during bad weather and fog. The suggestion of a lighthouse on this station was first put forward in 1885, but this was overruled by the Board of Trade. A lightship was placed on station on 7 June 1887. At the request of various interested parties, Trinity House had offered to supply a vessel on loan until the Scottish authorities had built their own – the *North Carr*, in July 1889. She had a wooden hull made of oak and teak and was 103 feet in length, 23 feet 6 inches broad with a tonnage of 155. The crew consisted of the Master, Mate and nine seamen, of whom one officer and six seamen were always on board. 'The Master received £115.10.7d per year with uniform; the Mate £97.0.7d per year with uniform and the seamen £69.6.8d per year with uniform.'

It was a condition of their employment that the officers and crew resided in Crail, and when ashore to occupy themselves in a store, which had been built there for coke, provisions etc (the coke which was delivered to Crail Store at 27/- per ton was required to drive fog signal machinery on the light vessel). It was a further duty for the officer and three crew members ashore to man the Attending Boat, which sailed weekly for the Isle of May and fortnightly to the North Carr. To help this arrangement Alex Watson, Isle of May Boatman, was appointed Mate of the North Carr Lightvessel; Mr John Kirkpatrick, Boatswain, 'Pharos' was appointed Master.[80]

The lamp on this vessel was similar to Stephenson's design and it consisted of eight independent lamps, all mounted on gimbals and lit by colza oil. Her light was not distinct enough for those seafarers using the Forth and they complained about this but were informed that the lightship had been placed primarily as a fog signal ship. The light was only to prevent the lightship herself being run into. By 1910 the old light had been replaced with a new one fuelled by acetylene gas which alternated red and green. The old fog signal equipment was also replaced by a compressed air siren.

The *North Carr* lightship.
(Timweather)

The original wooden ship was replaced on 3 April 1933 by an iron- and steel-hulled vessel costing £15,430. Her hull and superstructure was painted red and the name *North Carr* painted on both sides of the hull. When first built she exhibited a fixed white beacon, but later this was replaced with a signal of two flashes in quick succession every half a minute, which could be seen over 10 miles away. The men on board were visited every two weeks for the delivery of rations, mail and crew reliefs. The crew of this new vessel consisted of 'one Senior Master, one Assistant Master, three Senior Enginemen, three Assistant Enginemen and 3 seamen'. The two Masters spent two weeks on board and two weeks ashore alternatively; others spent one month on board and two weeks ashore. Later the crew consisted of eleven men: one Senior Master, one Assistant Master, three Senior Enginemen, three Assistant Enginemen and three Seamen, of whom one Master, two Senior Enginemen, two Assistant Enginemen and two Seamen on board at the one time. During the Second World War she was moved to a station between the Mull of Kintyre and the Mull of Galloway, marking the entrance to the Clyde. She was refitted in 1952 when toilets and a radio beacon were also installed. This vessel was sold to the North East Fife District Council in July 1976 and was used as a floating museum moored in Anstruther harbour. She was based in Victoria Dock, Dundee and is used by the Maritime Volunteer Service.

The *North Carr* and the Broughty Ferry lifeboat disaster

The new steel and iron vessel was involved in one of the country's most tragic lifeboat disasters. In December 1959, the east coast of Scotland was experiencing one of the strongest storms in recorded history. A number of ships had been wrecked and crews lost. Given its position, the *North Carr* was particularly vulnerable in bad weather. Her mooring system was a single anchor weighing about 3 tons, and her riding cable was about 255 fathoms of linked chain designed to hold a ship over three times the weight of the vessel. On 8 December she was rolling and pitching heavily in a strong wind and very heavy seas. The anchor cable parted and as a result the helpless vessel drifted and was pushed almost onto her side at the height of the storm. Part of the cable was dragging along the seabed, which slowed the drift down. At 2.50 a.m. the crew of the lightship managed to deploy the port emergency anchor and eventually brought the vessel to a halt, but the situation remained extremely perilous.

At 2.20 a.m. the Fifeness coastguard noticed *North Carr* moving off station. At about the same time the Broughty Ferry lifeboat, the *Mona*, prepared to launch in order to come to the aid of the lightship. She was capable of being launched in any weather and was a veteran of many rescues. She was launched on what was to be her last rescue attempt at 3.13 a.m. The vessel was found on the morning of 9 December washed up on Buddon Sands near Carnoustie, with eight crew still inside. The body of the ninth crew member was never found.

On the stricken lightship the emergency cable parted, but eventually the crew were able to deploy their starboard anchor with 140 fathoms of cable. By this time the vessel was only about 1 mile from the rocky beach. Attempts to rescue the crew continued and they were eventually evacuated by the Royal Air Force in the early afternoon of the Wednesday 9 December. The rescue was made in extremely bad weather conditions. A full gale was blowing and the vessel was rolling and pitching heavily. To help rescue operations the crew cut away the 40-foot after mast. This action allowed the helicopters to fly very low above the lantern and pick up members of the crew from the charthouse roof. When the weather conditions had improved the crew was able to get back aboard the *North Carr* to allow her to be towed to the dockyards at Leith. The light vessel was eventually taken in tow by the Admiralty tug *Earner* on 11 December, repaired at Leith and put back on station on 16 March 1960. In the galley of the *North Carr* there was a simple brass plaque commemorating the loss of crew of the *Mona* in their fearless attempt to save the crew of the lightship.

The lifeboat *Mona*, 1910. (Author's Collection)

CHAPTER 12

Irish Lightships

Keepers were also allowed to carry on their trades, and keep a public-house in the lighthouse as was the case at Howth and Wicklow. At the Hook Tower the keeper was also a herb-doctor.

Early beginnings

The care and maintenance of lighthouses and lightships round the coast of Ireland has passed through the hands of a number of individuals and institutions over the centuries. In 1665, Charles II first imposed a levy on ships that used Irish ports to support the maintenance of six lighthouses about the coast. The Earl of Abercorn was granted a patent to maintain the lighthouses and collect the levies. He did not carry out these duties very satisfactorily and the patent was revoked in 1703. By this date only two lighthouses were working efficiently. Merchants and shipowners complained to the House of Commons that the levies imposed by the private lighthouse owners were a heavy burden on trade. After 1704, all lighthouses in Ireland that had been in private hands were transferred to the 'Revenue or Barrack Board,' and 'afterwards transferred to the Corporation for Preserving and Improving the Port of Dublin' who were also requested to build a new lighthouse in Dublin bay.[81] The Barrack Board contented itself with contracting the lights out to a contractor, who employed the keepers and paid all the expenses of maintenance. 'The pay given to light-keepers was very small, generally averaging £15 per annum but they were also given 'perquisites … of all the unburned portions of the candles'. Keepers were also allowed to carry on their trades, and keep a public house in the lighthouse as was the case at Howth and Wicklow. At the Hook Tower the keeper was also a herb doctor. In 1871 it was said that 'The Irish lighthouse service is now … quite adequately organized.'[82]

The Dublin Ballast Committee, a committee of Dublin Corporation set up by the Irish Parliament in 1708 (The Ballast Office Act 1707) became responsible for the Port of Dublin. Later, an Act of Parliament of 1763 instituted the 'Corporation for Preserving and Improving the Port of Dublin, to maintain and improve the Port'. This body was independent of Dublin Corporation. Its members were not seafarers, with the exception of one retired naval officer who had previously commanded the Irish coastguard. An 1810 Act of Parliament transferred the responsibility for the maintenance of all Irish lighthouses to the Ballast Board or the Corporation for Preserving and Improving the Port of Dublin. A number of lights had already been established about the Irish Coast at Howth, Balbriggan Pier, South Rock, Copeland Island, Aran More, Clarke Island, Loophead, Old Head Kinsale, Hook Head, Duncannon Fort and Wicklow Head.

The Ballast Board had purchased a steamer in 1851 to relieve Irish lighthouses, but this was removed from them in 1854 by the British Board of Trade, as they felt that it was not sufficiently used. The steamer was transferred to Trinity House and as a result the Ballast Board had to supply stores and crew to its lighthouses in local sailing vessels and make their inspections in steamers borrowed from Trinity House. As a consequence of this, stores and repairs were delayed and this in some instances endangered the very existence of the lights. When the Port of Dublin took over they found lighthouses to be in a very bad state of repair, some were derelict and others had broken lenses and leaking structures. By 1854, the Port of Dublin Corporation had become responsible for all the lights about the Irish coast with the proviso that they took advice from Trinity House, London, on the establishment of lightships or the building of any new lights. The developments that began in 1854 were completed by the Dublin Port Act of 1867, which established the 'Commissioners of Irish Lights'. The Merchant Shipping Act of 1894 later enacted that the commissioners must submit schemes for the erection of, or changes in, seamarks to Trinity House for their approval.

The Port of Dublin

The constant movement of tides about the coast of Ireland results in the build-up of sandbanks, which then become serious dangers to shipping. These moving sandbanks mean that many entrances to a number of Irish harbours have always been hazardous places for shipping. Dublin, Cork and Wexford Ports are particular examples. Dublin, a large shipping port since the early 1700s, was rather shallow, and this danger was, and still is, compounded by numerous sandbanks. In the past the port could only have been approached at high tide and was described in the early 1700s as the worst port in 'her Majesty's dominion'. Thousands of shipwrecks have been recorded over the years on the sandbanks in the bay. The entrance to Dublin harbour is particularly shallow at the bar, eastward to Poolbeg lighthouse; the depth of water over this sandbank in the early 1700s was only 6 feet at low water. The channel was later improved by 1717 and a new quay built. The first attempt to improve the port in 1707 was an Act of Parliament that vested powers in Dublin City to levy a small fee on ships entering the harbour. Later, a Committee of Dublin Corporation was entrusted by Parliament with the responsibility of maintaining and developing the port.

Palmers Light: Ireland's first lightship, 1736

In 1736 the first Irish lightship was stationed in Dublin bay and named *Palmers Light*, after James Palmer who managed the vessel that, 'being a small sloop, with a lantern at her mast head', was placed where the 'wall from what is now called the Pigeon-house to Ringsend began'. In 1704 it was proposed that a lighthouse should be sited at Poolbeg and to be lit by lamps rather than coal, which was the norm for other lighthouses. The seas at this site would have extinguished the light fuelled by coal, and there was a call for the 'lights to be kept in the lighthouse at Poolbeg should be large lamps: for this house standing in the sea, the waves beating violently against the underwork might extinguish a coal fire, and the light of the lamps (36 in number) would be more steady and constant, and cast a much greater light, and require much less attendance than any coal fire, and it was presumed would not be more expensive.'[83] The lightship was later removed on the completion of Poolbeg lighthouse, which had been funded by the Dublin Ballast Office and a grant from Parliament.

Palmers Light was a Gabbard, a flat-bottomed boat, carrying two lanterns, one lantern on each side of the yardarm on her single mast lit by candles at night. The candles were supplied by chandler Charles Wilcocks of Dublin. The light was looked after by four attendants paid between £10 and £18 per annum. The first attendant was appointed on 16 March 1744:

Four persons attended the light: First Hand @ £18 per annum, Second Hand @ £16 per annum, and 'two lusty boys' @ £10 each per annum. On 16 March 1774

The *Dudgeon* lightship. This was a similar type of vessel to *Palmers Light* in Dublin bay. (Author's Collection)

The Poolbeg lighthouse that replaced *Palmers Light*. It sits at the end of the south wall, which extends 4 miles out into Dublin bay. The original tower was built in 1768 and was redesigned and rebuilt in its present form in 1820. (Giuseppe Milo)

Thomas Risebron was appointed First Hand of the Floating Light, John Garnett Second Hand, William Rafferty Third Hand, and James Deane Fourth Hand. On the 3 August 1751, however, Risebron made a complaint against Rafferty. Rafferty was discharged and a 'proper hand' was ordered to be put in his place.

The crew cooked all their meals, on coal, on board and were paid a supplement during winter to purchase provisions. In winter 1749 all of the crew were 'issued with heavy fur coats to keep the weather out when on watch. Each coat cost £2.2s.'[84]

The lightship was damaged by another vessel in January 1743, and in April of that year she dragged her anchor and was washed up on rocks at nearby Dun Laoghaire harbour, considerably damaged. She was replaced by a temporary light and was refloated three months later in July. She was eventually replaced by the Poolbeg lighthouse in 1767.

The Kish Bank

Up to 1810 the only Irish lightship was *Palmers Light*, but in 1811 a second vessel was considered and placed on the Kish Bank, south-east of Dublin bay. The Kish Bank had always been marked by two large buoys at either end but, in darkness, vessels running into Dublin port could not safely navigate. Many attempting to do so not infrequently lost their passage and put themselves in danger. The Corporation for Preserving and Improving the Port of Dublin decided that it could be possible to place and maintain a floating light on the Kish Bank to make navigation much safer during darkness. The vessel *Veronia Gesina* of 103 tons was purchased, fitted out as a floating light, and was on station by November 1811. This was the first Irish vessel equipped for the purpose. She was named *Richmond* after the Lord Lieutenant who had originally requested that a lightship be placed on the Kish station. The *Richmond* cost £1,500, had three 'lanthorns' (sic) or lanterns, one on each mast, the centre mast being 3 feet higher than the other two. The lanterns slid up and down the mast in a groove and were hoisted by the crew. The centre lantern was heavier than the other two and was, when elevated, 6 feet higher. She was moored by a mushroom anchor, a design which allowed the vessel to swing freely and to ride easy by accommodating the length of the cable to the height and strength of the waves and the swell of the sea.[85] The greater the sea, the more cable is laid out to prevent the possibility of any sudden jerk raising the anchor and placing strain on the cable. The anchor chain, when fully set out, was over 250 fathoms.

The *Richmond* was manned by fourteen seamen, seven of whom served on board at any one time. In foggy weather a gong was sounded, and when the Holyhead Packet was expected an 18-pounder gun was also sounded. On occasion this did not prove of much use as she was often damaged by passing vessels, for example in October 1826 by the Steam Packet out of Liverpool. Earlier in 1821, the *Richmond* had broken her mooring, drifted, and ended up in Holyhead Port.[86] She had resumed her station by February 1822 but was withdrawn and broken up in 1827. The second lightship stationed on the Kish Bank was again run down by the mail boat RMS *Leinster* in September 1902. A lightship was positioned on this station until November 1965, when it was replaced by a lighthouse.

In December 1859 the Ballast Office of Dublin responded to representation from seafarers who argued that the three lights exhibited on the *Kish* lightship, when end on, were liable to be mistaken for a single fixed light. After consideration it was agreed that, from July 1860, the light exhibited from the foremast of the lightship was to be lowered 6 feet and exhibited at a height of 20 feet. The light exhibited on the mizen mast would also be lowered 5 feet and that on the main mast remained at the same height of 36 feet above the sea. This was 16 feet above the level of the other two lights. The lightship was also to carry a black ball, as a day mark, at each of her mastheads.[87] Similar changes were made to the lights exhibited on the *Blackwater Bank* lightship and the *Arklow Bank* vessel. The fixed light exhibited by the *Arklow Bank* vessel was changed to a bright revolving light that attained it greatest brilliance once in every minute and was exhibited from the main mast at a height of 39 feet above the sea.

The RMS *Lenister* passing the *Kish Bank* lightship in Dublin bay. She struck the *Kish* lightship in 1902. Operated by the City of Dublin Steam Packet Company, she served as the Kingstown–Holyhead mailboat until she was torpedoed and sunk by German submarine *UB-123* on 10 October 1918. (Author's Collection)

Provisioning Irish lightships

The Irish Lights service was financed by a general toll upon the tonnage of all vessels entering any Irish port. Before 1860, Irish lighthouses and lightships were not provided with 'meteorological instruments or medicine chests, lightning conductors, books, call whistles, printed regulations, uniforms for the men, clocks or dials or with anything not absolutely required for keeping the light burning and the apparatus clean'. The Irish lighthouse service never had a history of providing out of their revenue any financial support for poor seamen or their families, but after 1860 crews were supplied with uniforms. The following notice was placed in the *Dublin Evening Mail* in September 1860, inviting tenders for the provision of clothing:

> Notice
> Port of Dublin Corporation are willing
> To receive Proposals from competent parties for the supply of
> Uniform Clothing for the Light keepers and Light-Ship men in their
> Service, as follows:-
> 'About 120 Light Keepers' Suits
>   '12 masters and Mates' do
>   '40 Light-Ship men's' do
>   '10 Seamen's' do
> Patterns may be inspected at this Office any day between the hours
> of 12 and 3 o'clock up to SATURDAY, the 29th Inst.
> Sealed Tenders stating price per Suit, accompanied by Samples of
> Cloth, duly labelled, will be received at this Office up to 4 o'clock on
> WEDNESDAY, the 3rd proximo.
> The Corporation do not bind themselves to accept the lowest
> Tender.   By Order.   W. LEES Secretary
> Ballast Office, Dublin. 22nd September. 1860

Later in the nineteenth century lightship men were paid about £105 per year, but they would have had to purchase their own frock or jacket, trousers and cap – costing in total about 20 shillings. Irish lightship men had always to provision their stay on board themselves when on station.

CHAPTER 13

The Dangerous Wexford Coast – A Lightship Community

Blackwater Bank is simply a ship trap which may be regarded as 'set' when a spring tide, a half ebb, and a dark night occur together.

The Wexford coast

The 150 miles or so of the Wexford coast has always been recognised as a very dangerous stretch of coastline; it is the graveyard of hundreds if not thousands of vessels. The coast is encumbered with dangerous sandbanks that are usually hidden beneath the waves. The weather comes predominantly from the Atlantic and December and January are usually the worst weather months, with June and July the best. Life on the east and south coast has always been lived in intimate contact with the sea. For hundreds of years, loss of life at sea was accepted as inevitable. But slowly, all too slowly, courageous men, shipowners and local seafarers spoke up and demanded action to save lives on this coast.

During darkness or in poor visibility, a ship's crew would not be able to see rocks or other obstacles in their path. The only way vessels would have been alerted to these hazards was with the aid of a lightship or lighthouse. The Master of the steamer *Brigand*, Henry Poole, wrote in September 1840 to the *Wexford Independent*, a local newspaper, about the dangers, uncertainty and difficulty of vessels avoiding the sand banks between Greenore Point in south Wexford and the Arklow Bank off its north coast. This journey was particularly hazardous at night and in bad weather. He spoke for many a seaman when he went on to say that, 'The only wonder is, that a matter of such vital importance should have so long remained without the special attention of those whose duty and interest it is to endeavour to prevent such dangers.'[88] He proposed to Trinity House that a lightship should at least be placed at the south-west end of the Blackwater Bank.

The first lightship placed on these sands was the *South Arklow*, stationed on the sandbank off the north Wexford coast, but further down this dangerous

The Blackwater station off the Wexford coast was established on 14 November 1857 and discontinued in 1968. (Jack Higginbotham)

coast there was no such aid to navigation. The Master of the *Brigand* also pointed out the particular dangers of vessels approaching the very busy Wexford port. Along with his proposal that a lightship be placed at the south-west end of the Blackwater Bank, he also encouraged those in authority in Ireland and the port of Liverpool to pressure Trinity House to consider the matter. Five years later the situation on this coast had not changed, which was as dangerous as ever to shipping. Francis Harpur, an agent for Lloyd's in Wexford, stated that at least four ships a year were lost on this coast to the value of £70,000. Another Lloyd's agent, William Powell, later stated that in the first half of the nineteenth century seventeen vessels were wrecked on the south Wexford coast.

The increasing demand for lightships on the Wexford coast

On 4 January 1863, the Wexford Harbour Commissioners, concerned about the amount of shipping lost on the banks, took evidence at its weekly meeting from Captain Nott, employed by Lloyd's underwriters. He reported that the Admiralty viewed the coast between Wexford and Dublin as being very dangerous. Captain Nott had previously carried out an enquiry into the loss of ships in the area and had concluded that it was not the weather that was the principal cause but the impossibility of seeing the ordinary lights and land marks on the coast. He argued for lightships to remedy the situation and also advocated that they should be fitted with danger signals and have a gun on board to be fired in bad weather or fog. He thought that six such vessels, with green lights, should be placed on the Arklow Bank and four on the Blackwater Bank. Admiral Hamilton, Nott's superior, disagreed with his opinion, because of cost, and proposed bell buoys rather than lightships. It cost £6,000 to build and equip a lightship with £1,300 running cost each subsequent year. The Wexford Harbour Commissioners, however, supported Captain Nott's argument and were glad to hear later that a commission had been appointed to take evidence on the subject. Only one lightship was added despite the fact that 'the light revenues of this Kingdom actually exceed the expenditure by £50,000 or £60,000 per annum, such a piece of extravagance was not thought of either by 'my Lords', Elder Brethren or Honourable Ballasters'. Captain Nott's arguments were considered by Trinity House to be 'troublesome suggestions', despite many believing that the 'Blackwater Bank is simply a ship trap which may be regarded as 'set' when a spring tide, a half ebb, and a dark night occur together. Woe betide the ship that nears it on such occasion, and God help the widows and children of the brave sailors who are allowed by the stupidity of others to drift thus on certain death.'[89]

The matter was left unresolved for a number of years, which caused great concern as ships continued to be lost each year on this coast. The promised inquiry into the dangers of navigating the Wexford coast and harbour was not held until some years later in 1866. Robert Hunte, who commanded a steamer out of Wexford, stated that he would never navigate out of or into Wexford port at night because of the dangers. Without lights, he commented, it would be very dangerous to run in. He usually, when sailing from Bristol, stood off near the Tuskar until daylight before attempting to enter the harbour. Evidence offered to the 1886 enquiry commented that ships could have been saved if at least one lightship had been stationed at the south end of the Blackwater Bank. It had been rumoured that the lightship stationed on the 'Coneybeg' (sic) would be placed on the Blackwater when the proposed lighthouse was erected to replace that lightship. The *Coneybeg* or *Coningbeg* had been placed near the Saltee Islands in 1824 to warn of the rock off the Brandies, named the *Conningmore* and *Coningbeg*. Captain Frazer RN, the Admiralty Surveyor on the coast of Ireland, did propose in 1824 a lightship to be placed on the Blackwater Bank, but this was not acted upon.

The *Petrel* on the Coningbeg station. A lightship was first placed on this station in 1824 and withdrawn in 1982. (Jack Higginbotham)

Wexford coast dangers and the *Wexford Independent*

Alderman John Green, JP, of Wexford Corporation had been pressing for lightships on the banks off the coast for over twenty years. Green was the owner of the local newspaper, the *Wexford Independent*, which had been established in 1769. Eventually in 1857, the Ballast Office, Dublin, informed him 'that a length of the dangerous shoal on our (Wexford) south east coast, known as the Blackwater Bank, shall have a lightship placed thereon from the first of October 1857.'[90] After support from Mr John Redmond, the local MP, a parliamentary enquiry and a blue book, the enquiry was published. Instead of commenting on the lack of lightships, the report defamed sailors, stating that all the shipwrecks on the banks were because 'sailors were in the habit of leaving Liverpool drunk'. Most of the ships wrecked in the mid-1800s had traded or sailed from the port of Liverpool. However, a lightship was eventually placed on this dangerous Blackwater Bank and two more were stationed later, the *Lucifer* on Wexford Bar and a vessel on the Barrels rock. The vessel at the Barrels was established in October 1880 after a ship had mistaken a nearby lightship, the *Coningbeg*, with its two fixed white lights for the Tuskar Rock lighthouse.

The Coney Rock, just off the Saltee Islands, had been marked by the *Coningbeg* lightship since 1824 after a number of failed attempts to establish a lighthouse on the rock. The Wicklow Swash was briefly marked by a lightship in 1865. The southern end of the Arklow Bank had already been marked by 1825. In 1867, a lightship was stationed to mark the Codling Bank, and the Lucifer Sandbank was marked the following year. Further south, the Barrels off Carnsore Point were marked in 1880. After the sinking of the *City of New York* liner on the Daunt Rock outside Cork harbour, a lightship was also stationed there in 1874, but this proved to be a very dangerous station. In 1896 the lightship *Puffin* foundered, with the loss of her full crew of eight lightship

The *Codling Bank* lightship. A lightship was first stationed on this bank in 1867 and discontinued in 1976. (Author)

men, and its replacement on this station, the *Gannet*, was hit by a large cargo ship in 1884. A third vessel on this station, the *Comet*, broke her moorings in 1936 and the crew were only rescued by the gallant efforts of the Ballycotton lifeboat. All lightships in the responsibility of the Commissioners of Irish Lights were painted black up to 1954, when the decision was made to paint them red so that they could be seen more easily against the coast.

The manning of the Irish lights – 'The Wexford Navy'

Wexford County has a history of providing seamen for local ships using the port since medieval times. Over the centuries seamen from the county gained a reputation in many ports and countries all over the globe for their seafaring prowess. Seamen from Wexford gained experience on deep-sea ships over many years before joining the lightship service. The more experienced had served on the old schooners that sailed from Wexford port. As a result, the County of Wexford produced a large number of men who manned the Irish lightships from the early 1800s. In April 1901 all the crew of the *Blackwater* vessel were from Wexford, all seven of the *Lucifer*'s crew were from the county. Six of the seven crew of the *Coningbeg* lightship and the *Barrels* were living in Wexford. Four of the crew of the *Skulmartin*, off the Northern Ireland coast, were also from the county. Ten years later there was little change. In April 1911, serving on the *Lucifer* lightship were six crew from Wexford, and on the *Blackwater* and *Barrels* all seven of the crew were from the area. The *Petrel* and *South Arklow* had at least two members of the crew from Wexford town. In 1911, of the total number employed in the Irish lightship service, 119, over 60 per cent, were from Wexford County. Between 1940 and 1945, over sixty-two Wexford men served in the service. By 1950 the number employed had fallen

A lightship was first placed on the Lucifer Sand bank 1867 and discontinued in 1939. (Jack Higginbotham)

to ninety-three, but more than 55 per cent were living in Wexford, a percentage which rose in 1967 to over 58 per cent. As the number of vessels in service fell, so did the number of men employed, and by 1972 only fifty-eight lightship men were in service and only 38 per cent were from Wexford.

These lightship men accepted long periods away from families and the hard dangerous work involved. In the early days of the service they spent six weeks on board and two ashore. Later, this became one month on board and one month ashore. During the winter months the time on board was sometimes determined by the weather and the ability of brave men who risked their lives in small vessels to relieve the lightship. One must also remember the pain and distress of lightship families during great storms, such as the one which occurred on the Wexford coast in October 1916. Local seafaring families remember it as the worst storm in living memory. The ferocity of the weather caused much damage in the town and the local coast. Many boats were lost and families must have thought and prayed hard for those on local lightships who could not run or seek shelter from the storm.

A number of lightship men paid with their lives while on board, some dying from injuries sustained from accidents, others from natural causes, such as William Delaney, from Wexford, who died on the *South Rock* in 1913; Captain Duff who died on the *Codling* and James Quirk who died on the *Lucifer* in 1933. In some cases whole crews disappeared, as when the *Puffin* was wrecked on Daunt Rock.

Difficulties of servicing and relieving vessels in bad weather on the Wexford coast

On a number of occasions the lightships stationed on the Wexford coast have been left without fresh provisions for many weeks because of bad weather. In February 1935, wild weather prevented the relief of the local lightships for over three weeks. During this period of heavy weather a number of large vessels had got into trouble and even large steamers, such as the *Cargan* of 272 tons, were towed into Rosslare harbour after a 25-hour battle with the heavy seas. Steam trawlers, coasters and large deep-sea tramp steamers were also forced into Rosslare Bay for shelter.

Marooned by the heavy seas, the crews of the lightships had been living on short rations and began to run out of emergency provisions. The crews had also begun to ration their fresh drinking water. They would have had little sleep as the vessels received a terrible battering from the gale. The crew, except the watch on some of the vessels, were confined below because of the danger of being washed overboard by the heavy seas. On 21 February the relief tender, despite sailing in brilliant sunshine, was unable to relieve the vessels as the gale blew

Capt. McCleane's provisions basket. This type of basket was used by all Irish lights crew to bring provisions on board. It was waterproof. Captain McCleane served on the Irish lightships for many years and was Master of the *South Rock*. On leaving the Irish lightships he had a distinguished career in the Merchant Marine service. (Neal McCleane)

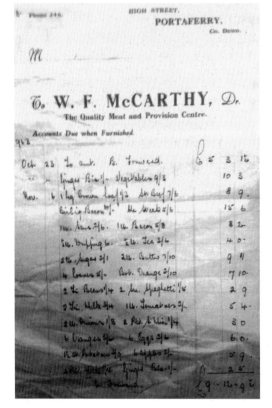

Photograph of a receipt dated November 1963 from a grocery store in Co. Down for supplies for Captain McCleane on joining the *Southrock* lightship. This had to last two weeks. (Captain McCleane)

very strong. In January 1937, a gale again lashed the Wexford coast for over a month, preventing any attempt to approach the *Blackwater*, *Barrels*, *Lucifer* and *Coningbeg* lightships. For over twenty-nine days the vessels could not be relieved and fresh provisions were reported to be exhausted. The crew were down to eating salt beef and 'hard tack', a type of hard biscuit softened by immersing in water or hot tea. Usually there were three months' supply of emergency rations on board. The Irish vessels at this period had no way of communicating any

Bringing the mail to the lightship
in heavy weather. (Author's
Collection)

difficulties or lack of provisions with other ships or shore except by signalling
passing vessels to pass on comments or requests after reaching port.

Later, in December 1946, the *Coningbeg* was nine days overdue to be relieved
because of heavy weather. A local tender from Kilmore Quay was called in to
relieve the lightship as the larger Irish Lights tender was unable to complete
the run. It was eventually carried out successfully. In January 1948, two years
later, the gales of the Wexford coast again prevented the relief tender from
providing supplies to the marooned crew of the *Coningbeg* lightship. The crew
had sufficient emergency provisions for some days but they had not been visited
since 20 December. Some of the crew had not been relieved for over sixty days.
A few weeks later, at the beginning of February 1948, very heavy weather
again prevented any relief for the *Coningbeg* for many days. The tender *Irene*,
although able to provision Tuskar Rock lighthouse, was unable to get near the
lightship for over twenty-two days. On the twenty-second day, after 4 hours
of battling against very heavy seas, the *Irene* was able to transfer the men and
provisions to and from the lightship. The launch of the tender used to carry out
the operation was swamped by the large waves many times before the transfer
was completed successfully.

CHAPTER 14

Irish Lightship Tragedies and Heroes

They showed a true Christian spirit by losing their lives in attempting to save the lives of others. These men were an honour to human nature and a credit to their country.
The Loss of a Lightship Rescue Crew, January 1865

The Arklow Bank on the east coast was a very hazardous station and also a very busy shipping lane. On this station lightships suffered a number of collisions and disasters over the years. On 6 January 1880 the *John Shelly* from Belfast collided with the lightship. Later, during a heavy gale in October 1896, she drifted 3 miles off station. Again, in November 1899, she dragged her anchors in heavy weather and again drifted off station[91]. In early October 1910 two vessels, the *Tayaden* and *The Marchioness*, collided with her – no lives were lost but one of the crew was seriously injured.

The loss of a lightship etc.

The *Armenian*, a British cargo steamer of 763 tons built in 1855, was under command of Capt. Thomas Leamon on 25 January 1865. She carried twenty-eight First Class passengers, two Second Class passengers and eight Deck passengers with a crew of forty. She had left Liverpool early on the 25th, and later that day the weather deteriorated and a heavy fog set in. In the course of the afternoon she stopped twice to take soundings. At midnight, when under full steam and canvas, she ran on the Arklow Bank and shortly afterwards fire broke out in the after deck house, which was soon extinguished by the heavy seas. The boats were got ready, one of which was found stove in, and the others were launched without mishap. During the night the foremast and the main topmast was carried away and the ship broke in two. The remaining passengers and crew, who had not managed to get into the lifeboats, took to the main and mizzen rigging. A steamship the *Montague* came to the rescue and picked up two of the *Armenian's* boats. Sometime previously, four men from the lightship had attempted to get to the wreck in a gig belonging to the *Armenian*, they had volunteered to go to the rescue of those seamen in the rigging of the wreck. When attempting the rescue, the lightship crew had to come round a point where there was violent surf. They were unable to clear the surf and the boat was swamped and its crew of four drowned. An eyewitness reported that the 'boat was also seen coming from the lightship under canvass and pulling, when within 100 yards of the wreck was drawn into the surf and swamped drowning the brave and humane fellows she contained, four in number, including Coghlan, the son of the chief boatman'.[92] The total loss of life was eight people, including the rescue party from the lightship. The *Armenian* was completely underwater, nothing of her being visible over water but her masts and topsails.

Sixty persons were taken on board the lightship and were then transported to nearby Wexford Port by the *Montague* under the command of Captain Clarke. When they reached Wexford the officers and ladies were accommodated in White's Hotel, and the rest of the crew were given shelter in houses in the town. The Ballast Board steamer *Princess Alexandria* went down to the *Arklow* lightship, but owing to the severe weather was only able to speak to her, and was not able to put four replacement men on board. The *Alexandra* returned to Kingstown without transferring the new crew to the lightship. The four crewmen were eventually replaced on Wednesday 1 February. Within a few days, over £130 had been collected locally for the families of the four crewmen. The newspapers commented on the bravery of the four crewmen. 'They showed a true Christian spirit by losing their lives in attempting to save the lives of others. These men were an honour to human nature and a credit to their country.'[93]

The disappearance and loss of the crew of a lightship at the Daunt Rock Cork harbour

The Daunt Rock is a reef about 5 miles off the coast of Cork. Vessels leaving Cobh and Cork Harbour needed to set course carefully to avoid this dangerous rock which had always been a hazard to shipping. Following the wreck of the *City of New York* in 1846 on the Rock, the Vice-President of the Board of Trade in 1868 was asked in Parliament if the government had considered placing a lighthouse on the rock because of the danger to naval as well as mercantile interests. In the autumn of 1846 the Ballast Board, later the Irish Lights Commissioners, changed the light of nearby Roche's Point Lighthouse into a red revolving light, throwing a sector of white light from the lighthouse across the Daunt Rock. It also established a bell-boat, all at the expense of the Mercantile Marine Fund.

As early as 1864 a lightship had been offered to Cork, but the city fathers felt they did not want passing ships paying levies as the cost might affect the economic viability of the port, so it was refused. Their danger was not so great, they felt, as to justify the Irish Lights Commissioners placing the financial burden compulsorily on the trade of Cork. John Francis Maguire, the illustrious Lord Mayor of Cork, founder and publisher of the *Cork Examiner* newspaper in 1841, later, with some foresight, wrote to *The Times* complaining about the delay in placing a light on the Daunt Rock, and pointing out that the proposed light bell would prove inadequate because of the large seas that occurred in the area. He went on to give his opinion of those who were inactive in supporting a floating light and of red tape:

> It is with reluctance that I venture again to trespass upon your space in reference to a matter which, I am ashamed to say, has still to be ultimately decided. I flattered myself with the belief that I should never again have to trouble you, or run the risk of boring your readers, with the subject of Daunt's Rock and its dangers; but when I formed this delusive hope I did not adequately appreciate the sublime imperturbability of redtapeism and routine. Humbly recognising its flow, after months of anxious expectation, I am filled with apprehension for the future, not knowing what disasters may result from a delay which, whatever the motives that inspired it, be they of the best, is as discreditable to our public departments as it is unaccountable on any reasonable grounds.[94]

On 19 March 1864, the *City of New York* left the USA for her regular voyage to Liverpool via Queenstown. Approaching Cork, the captain chose to take the inner passage between the Daunt Rock and the nearest headland, and was proceeding at about 14 knots when the ship grounded firmly on the rock. All on board were rescued, but the ship was stuck fast. After numerous attempts at salvage she slipped beneath the waves on 7 April. Two years later in April 1866, an unnamed Isle of Man fishing vessel, on passage from Cork to Kinsale passing the Rock, struck on one of the masts of the wrecked *City of New York* and began to sink. The Master ran her towards shore and she made it as far as Rocky Bay, where she sank. The crew of nine were saved.

In January 1864, the steam-powered iron-clad HMS *Research* was on patrol duties along the south coast of Ireland. Outside Cork harbour she signalled an American ship, the *Alaska*, to stop. This was ignored; HMS *Research* gave chase. On passing the Daunt Rock she came too close to the rock and became impaled on the wreck of the *City of New York*. Eventually, a lightship called the *Puffin* was placed at Daunt Rock in 1864.

The *Puffin* lightship 1896: lost with all hands

In December 1897 Captain Donelan, the Irish MP for East Cork, asked the President of the Board of Trade if the Irish Lights Board had made any provision for the widows and families of the men lost on the sinking of the *Puffin* lightship in October 1896. Captain Donelan was referring to the founding of the Daunt Rock lightship, the *Puffin*, in a severe south-south-westerly gale which blew with hurricane force on 8 October 1896, with the loss of all eight crewmen on board. The Commissioners of Irish Lights had applied for sanction to make payment to the families of those who died in this disaster.[95]

This area on the south coast of Ireland takes the full force of southerly and easterly gales. Such a severe gale had been blowing since the evening of 7 October and did not moderate until late afternoon on the day of the disaster. The lightship had been seen earlier in the day labouring heavily in the very high seas. The local coastguard had reported seeing the light at about 4.30 p.m. on that afternoon, about the same time that very heavy seas washed away parts of the local coast. Locals stated that they had never experienced such a sea in their lifetime. A pilot on nearby Roche's Point waiting to board a steamer had to have his pilot boat pulled up out of the harbour as the weather was so bad. This was the situation in which the *Puffin* disappeared. At daylight she could not be seen at her station and it was hoped that she had only broken her mooring and was adrift. A number of people thought they had sighted her but eventually it was accepted that she had foundered and her eight crew lost. It was not until Saturday the 10th that the Superintendent of Irish Lights arrived on site to supervise the operation to sweep the area to try and find the wreck of the *Puffin*. In the meantime it was arranged for another lightship, the *Guillemot*, to replace the *Puffin* on the Daunt Rock station.

The *Puffin* lightship, built in 1886/87 at a cost of £6,000. She was stationed on the Daunt Rock when she sank with the loss of all hands on 8 October 1896. (Jack Higginbotham)

The wreck of the *Puffin* at Rushbrook Cork harbour. (Author's Collection)

On Tuesday 21 October a diver discovered the cable of the *Puffin*, but because of bad weather it was not until a week later that the ship was discovered in 15 fathoms of water a little to the eastward of her usual station. No trace was found of the bodies of the crewmen. As with many Irish lightships, a number of the crew were from Wexford. Robert Higginbotham (listed incorrectly in the Board of Trade report as Robert Higgias), the carpenter, lived in Parnell Street; another eight members of Robert's family were also in the Irish Lights service. Laurence Furlong, who was also lost, lived in Parnell Street and was a neighbour of Robert Higginbotham. In local folklore the men of the *Puffin* remain at their post as a ghost ship, to warn other shipping of impending danger.

The Board of Enquiry heard that the *Puffin* was last seen at 4.30 a.m. on 8 October – no gun was heard or distress signal seen at any time. The hearing found that 'the cause of the founding of the vessel and loss of life was due to the steel mast breaking below the deck carrying away the house and tearing up a large portion of the deck in its fall. The area the hole made in the deck was about 20 feet, and would admit of enormous quantities of water getting below, so that undoubtedly the vessel would fill rapidly and founder.'[96] Whether the mast gave way first, causing the mast to lose its support owing to the excessive strain either by pitching and rolling about in the terrible cross sea that was on at the time, or whether she was struck by any wreckage, causing a sudden shock, which may have affected the masts, the court was unable to say.

The *Puffin* – like a number of lightships of the time such as the *Cormorant*, built in 1871, and *Torch*, built in 1880 – was constructed with a slender main mast carrying a 'hoistable' lantern and a fore and mizzen mast. The lantern weighed about 2 tons up a 30-foot mast. This mast design was unsafe and unsuitable for such a heavy lantern, and on later models this 'hoistable' design was converted into a fixed lantern. Many of the new Irish Light's vessels were redesigned after this incident.

Robert Higginbotham lost on the *Puffin*. (Jack Higginbotham)

After the inquiry into the loss of the *Puffin*, the Board of Trade wrote to Trinity House with a summary of the findings indicating that the disaster was due to the breaking of the main mast which tore up a large portion of the deck. The board pointed out that the Irish Lights Commissioners intended to introduce a stronger type of steel mast on some existing and all future vessels. The Board of Trade requested the observation of Trinity House on this proposal. No reply to their request has been found and there is no evidence that Trinity House ever reconsidered the design of their existing lightships.

The lightship stationed on this rock was again involved in an incident in February 1936 when the lightship *Daunt Rock* drifted and broke her moorings during a severe storm. As when the original vessel the *Puffin* disappeared, a number of Wexford men were on the lightship. The lightship broke from her moorings during a severe storm. The weather was so bad and concern for the crew so great that the Ballycotton lifeboat stood by the lightship for three days, as did a British Navy vessel, *Tenedo*. The anchor held and there were no casualties.

Leaving the scene of a collision with a lightship 1901

Just over thirty year later, on 28 November 1901, during heavy weather and fog the *Arklow* lightship was run down by a ship out of Liverpool, the *Aigburth* – an iron full-rigged vessel. In the collision the main mast of the lightship was carried away, but the *Aigburth* did not stop to ascertain if any of the lightship's crew needed help or if the vessel was in danger. Three steamers from Queenstown (Cobh) were despatched to find the offending ship and escort her back to port in order that an investigation could take place. She was located two days later and towed into Queenstown. The Court of Inquiry into the accident was held in Cork on 17 January 1902 and lasted five days. After listening to all the evidence, the enquiry found that the collision with the lightship was due to negligent navigation by Captain John Henry Reid. His certificate was suspended for three months. In giving evidence the ship's captain had tried to blame an inaccurate compass for the disaster, but this was found to be working later when he carried on his original course. It was also found that a proper lookout had not been kept.

The court heard that the *Aigburth*, after founding on the Arklow Bank, had drifted towards the lightship, striking her a sliding blow, and had 'fouled the lantern mast with her fore and fore-topsail braces and jib boom guys carrying the mast with its lantern and rigging over the side, and doing other damage.'[97] The *Aigburth*, after drifting past the lightship, just repaired her braces and other damage, and proceeded on her voyage without attempting to communicate with the lightship. The court and local press were horrified to find that after the collision the captain had not stood by to ascertain if the lightship required assistance. The *Aigburth* was later wrecked in 1904 on a previously uncharted coral reef off Rook Island, New Guinea, still under command of Captain Reid. The crew left the ship in four boats and three reached safety. One of the boats with the second Mate and seven men were lost.

The sinking of the *Albatross*: Kish Bank 1902

The lightships on the Kish station have always being prone to being run down by passing vessels, and in particular the *Mail Packet* from Holyhead to Dublin. A fog signal was always sounded when the *Packet* was due to pass the lightship. The Ballast Office became so concerned by the danger to the lightship that they issued detailed instructions to the lightship in March 1865 as to the use of fog signals:

> The following alterations will take place in the time for firing the fog gun on board the light-vessel at the Kish Bank, to indicate to the Morning and Evening Mail Packets from Holyhead, the position of the light-vessel and that the said gun will in future be discharged during Foggy Weather in the manner following, vis:- For the mooring and evening mail, Two discharges in quick succession, commencing at 6 a.m. and 5 p.m., to be continued every 15 minutes for three hours, if in the meantime the mail Packet has not passed or the fog cleared off, when such firing will cease; if after the expiration of the three hours, should a gun be fired from the Mail Packet , on the signal being heard on board the light ship, she will fire two guns in quick succession in answer to such signal.[98]

However, on the afternoon of 8 September 1902 there was a thick fog at the Kish Bank. The RMS *Leinster* had almost completed her journey from Holyhead to Kingstown, but in the reduced visibility she rammed and sank the wooden Kish Bank lightship the *Albatross*. The lightship fog guns were sounding but the captain of the *Leinster* had not seen or heard the lightship until he was about half the steamer's length away. There was no loss of life and the Master and all seven

This is a group of lightship men on an unknown Irish lightship. Note the large fog gun or carranode, which would have operated during fog. (Jack O'Leary)

crew members of the *Albatross*, having lowered one of their own boats, were taken on board the *Leinster*. One of the crew had been asleep when the lightship was struck and the boat had to return to rescue him. William Daly, the Master of the *Albatross*, said that two fog guns had been fired every 8 minutes. The Master later commended his men for their courage and coolness. No man had showed any nervousness and they only went for their boat when he gave the order. As the lightship did not appear to be sinking as quickly as he first thought, he allowed some of the crewmen back onto the ship for their belongings.[99] The damage to the lightship was estimated to be over £30,000. The lightship later sank about 5 p.m. in 13 fathoms and was replaced by a temporary vessel the following day. The *Leinster* sailed for Holyhead the following morning having suffered no more than a few dents on her bow plates. There was no formal investigation under the Merchant Shipping Act as the case was likely to be heard in the Admiralty Court. The Board of Trade refused to support any formal investigation as they were not prepared to incur the expense of detaining witnesses for any inquiry. The owners of the *Lenister* later admitted liability for running into the lightship.

The *Barrels* incident 1905

The *Barrels* lightship stationed off Carnsore Point was driven from her mooring in very bad weather in March 1905. The weather forced the lightship to drag her moorings. After some time the crew managed to deploy the second anchor, just in time, as they were drifting towards Tuskar Rock. The vessel was buffeted about so violently with heavy seas breaking over the deck, two members of the crew were injured. When the weather abated the lightship was towed to safety. The two crew who had been seriously injured were taken ashore for treatment. The vessel was later towed back to her station by the lightship tender *Moya* and a new anchor fitted. During the Second World War the *Barrels* lightship was withdrawn because of the danger of attack by German planes. She was replaced with a new vessel in November 1949.

The *Barrels* lightship was first placed on station in October 1880. Note that it has the same mast type and lantern as the ill-fated *Puffin*. During the Second World War she was withdrawn because of the danger of attack by German planes and replaced by a buoy. (Jack Higginbotham)

The lightship *Osprey* and *Guillemot* 1917 – light signals are almost valueless in thick fog

In 1902 the South Arklow Bank lightship, the *Osprey*, was damaged by a passing sailing vessel. The newspapers offered the opinion 'that such accidents seem to show that signals are almost valueless in thick fog.'[100] In 1917 the South Arklow lightship, the *Guillemot*, was involved in an incident with the German navy. By 1917 the war at sea was not going well for the German navy. Kaiser Wilhelm ordered that the Ubootwaffe, an elite submarine unit, carry out unrestricted attacks on neutral and allied ships in the Irish Sea, later to become known as U-Boat Ally. The United Kingdom had been running out of food, money, munitions and ships at an alarming rate which caused great distress to Great Britain and almost brought the country to its knees. The situation only became less acute when America entered the war in April 1917. One U-boat in particular, *UC-65*, wreaked havoc on shipping about the Irish Channel and the south coast of England. This particular submarine destroyed 105 ships and damaged a further twelve (a total of 192,780 tons).

One of the vessels sunk by *UC-65* was the Irish lightship *Guillemot* on 28 March 1917. The *Guillemot* had witnessed a number of sinkings by *UC-65* in the hours leading up to the incident, one of which was the *Harvest Home* a small schooner out of Wexford. The Master of the lightship, James Rossiter from nearby Wexford town, was an experienced lightship man. He had joined the service after some years at sea and served on the *North Arklow*, the *Daunt*, *Coldlin*, *Coningbeg* and finally the *South Arklow*. On 28 March he noticed that a large ship was approaching and he felt obliged to warn her that a U-boat was in the area. He ran up the signal to indicate this and also fired warning rockets. The vessel the *Annan* turned about to the north-east and escaped. The captain of the U-boat observed this action, surfaced, and ordered the lightship to be abandoned. The crew lowered a boat and were ordered to come alongside the U-boat. The crew of the U-boat placed two large bombs on the lightship, and,

The South Arklow lightship, *Guillemot*, scuttled by German U-boat *UXC-65* on 28 March 1917. She was launched in November 1893 and cost £7,900. (Author's Collection)

after attempting to remove her large bell, they lit bomb fuses which exploded some 10 minutes later. The lightship did not sink immediately and was shelled some hours later by the U-boat.

The lightship crew were later picked up by the very ship that they had warned and were landed at Wicklow on the morning of the 29th. All of the crew were from Wexford, Captain Rossiter and Peter Gadderen were from the Faythe, Patrick Cogley, School Street, Patrick Sinnott, Courtown, Martin Murphy, King Street and John Leader from Green Street. Captain Rossiter was later highly commended for his actions. He and his crew were awarded the 'Torpedo Badge' by King George V in September 1918. This was a new award created to be conferred on those who had risked their lives in the performance of their duty at sea.[101]

The sunk *Guillemot* was replaced in 1923 by a new vessel, also named *Guillemot*. Her main lantern was fitted on top of a steel mast. A single ball day marker was placed on the top of the tall mizen mast. Watertight bulkheads divided her hull into six compartments. The first forward compartment was used for storage of deck gear. The next compartment, the larger, was used for the crew's quarters and was lined with teak. It was fitted out with a stove, gallcy range, bread tanks, lockers for clothes and hammocks. The fifth compartment was fitted out as the Mate and Master's quarters with panelling of polished

A German U-boat similar to the one that sunk the *South Arklow* lightship. (Author's Collection)

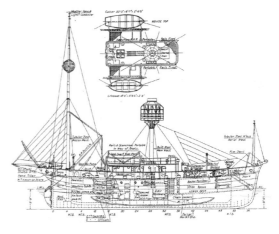

Drawing of the lightship *Guillemot*, built to replace the *South Arklow* which was scuttled by a German U-boat in 1917. (Author)

mahogany. The last compartment aft was used for storage of paint and rope. On deck was a large steel deckhouse which embraced all companionways designed so that no member of the crew had to be exposed to bad weather. The deckhouse also contained workshops, the lamp trimming room and lockers for flags and rockets. On deck the anchor chains were handled by a large windlass controlled by a compressed air plant. The bilge keels were of a special design. The weight was distributed in such a way as to give maximum radius of gyration without reducing stability.

The lightship *Comet* and the Ballycotton lifeboat rescue 1936

On 7 February 1930, rain, snow and wind was causing mountainous waves and destruction on the south coast of Ireland. The gale was blowing with unabated fury and on land it had inflicted serious damage uprooting trees and bringing down telephone wires. All communications between local communities and the outside world were severed. On the morning of 8 February, around 8 a.m., the black-hulled lightship *Comet*, on the Daunt Rock, sent out a distress signal indicating that she had broken her moorings and was drifting. She had experienced at least three days of very bad weather and was shipping heavy seas. The portable fire pump had fallen overboard in the heavy swell. The *Comet* had managed to anchor about a quarter of a mile off her station with her 'off station' lights lit. It was clear that she was in great danger, massive seas were rushing over her and the crew had not slept for at least 48 hours. Not only was the lightship in grave danger to herself but she was also a danger to other shipping because she had drifted off station.

Without any hesitation the coxswain of the Ballycotton lifeboat launched. The lifeboat, *Mary Stanford*, arrived at the rock, where she found other ships standing by. It was reported that stones, some a ton in weight, were being torn from the quay and flung like lumps of sugar in Ballycotton harbour. When the lifeboat reached the lightship the weather was so severe they could not approach the heavy vessel which was being tossed about by the waves. The crew had decided to stay on the lightship to continue marking the rock even though it was felt that the anchor might not hold. As the evening progressed the *Comet* began to drift towards the rock and the lifeboat crew, seeing this, began to pull alongside to try and get a steel cable aboard to tow her out of danger. Every time a cable was got aboard the heavy sea caused it to break. The lifeboat crew decided to leave the area to get stronger cables at the nearby harbour of Cobh. The crew of the lifeboat also took this opportunity to eat and get 3 hours sleep.

When the lifeboat returned the sea was still stormy and heavy fog was now also making any rescue more difficult. It became impossible to effect a rescue that day and the lightship continued to drift closer to the rock, a situation which, if the anchor cable broke, would mean that the vessel would be quickly dashed upon the rocks and the crew lost. The weather began to deteriorate further and the lightship's forward light was carried away by a large sea. By the evening the coxswain of the lifeboat decided that the crew had to be taken off urgently as she was moving wildly in the big seas. The coxswain made a number of attempts to allow the crew to jump onto the lifeboat and after the sixth attempt the last two exhausted crewmen were dragged aboard. Three Wexford men served on the vessel during this incident, B. Swift, John Murphy and James Busher. The crew of the lightship were taken to Cobh harbour. After 79 hours at sea the lifeboat returned to Ballycotton. The coxswain of the lifeboat was awarded the gold medal, the silver was awarded to the second coxswain and senior mechanic and bronze medals were awarded to the rest of the crew.

The next morning the lightship was boarded by the existing crew and was towed to Cobh where repairs were quickly carried out and she was back on station the following day. The lightship *Comet* had been built in 1904 in Glasgow. She was sold by the Irish Lights Commissioners in 1965 and ended up as a radio broadcasting station in Scotland.

Irish casualties during the emergency 1940–45

The Irish Lightship service, although operating from a neutral country, also suffered casualties during 1940–45. On 19 December 1940 the Irish Lights tender *Isolda*, a relief tender of the Commissioners of Irish Lights, left Rosslare harbour to carry a relief crew to the *Barrels* and *Coningbeg* lightships off the south Wexford coast. The *Isolda* was clearly marked with the words Lighthouse Service painted on the hull in letters 6 feet high. She also flew the blue ensign and had *Eire* painted on her hull. The tender had relieved the *Barrels* lightship and was on course to relieve the *Coningbeg*. About mid-morning a German plane dropped the first bombs on the ship. The plane swept across the *Isolda* from port to starboard dropping a number of bombs. The plane attacked the vessel at least three times, inflicting heavy damage. According to the report of the captain the tender was severely damaged and, realising that the ship was sinking, he gave the order to abandon ship. The vessel sank about 20 minutes after the crew had abandoned her. Six members of the crew were lost and seven wounded in the attack. The survivors made their way to Kilmore Quay, where the wounded were treated by the local doctor and later sent to Wexford County Hospital.

In 1941, during the Second World War, many of the lightships on the Wexford coast were withdrawn. The *Coningbeg* was the only lighted vessel left on station during this period. Lightships worked in constant danger of being damaged or sunk by mines that had broken from their moorings. At least twenty-one were washed up on one small part of the south Wexford coast in 1941. Many lightship men of the period talk of nervously watching as loose mines passed their ships with the flowing tide.

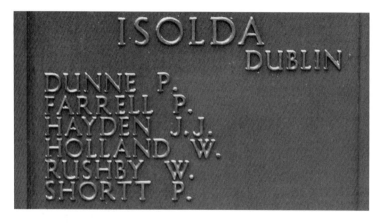

The Trinity House memorial on Tower Hill, London. The names of the men lost on the *Isolda* in 1941. (Author)

The Irish Lights Commissioners' steamer *Isolda*, sunk by German planes in 1940. She was first in service in 1928. (Author's Collection)

Heroic rescue by Michael Higginbotham *Coningbeg* lightship 1939

In February 1939 newspapers reported a 'Heroic rescue from Lightship – Injured man taken off in gale – Ships Mate accompanies him in small boat – Heroism by a member of a lightship crew was revealed to day.'

During 11 February 1939 a fierce south-westerly gale blew on the south Wexford coast. A number of ships had reported seeing distress signals in mountainous seas. On Sunday 12th, in this heavy weather a member of the crew of the lightship *Coningbeg* off the Wexford coast, William Gaddren, fell down a hatchway and was seriously injured. The lightship was rolling on her beam-ends and large seas were breaking all over her. His injuries necessitated medical treatment urgently. The lightship put out a distress rocket but because of the severe heavy weather passing steamers, who stood by the lightship, could not attempt a rescue. The passing ships were informed by the lightship's Master, Captain Quirke, by using Morse, of the injured man's serious condition. As the lightship had no wireless the passing steamers radioed SOS messages, which were picked up by local stations. The Irish lights steamer, *Irene*, was at nearby Rosslare harbour but could not put to sea because of the weather. The local Rosslare lifeboat coxswain James Wickham courageously launched in the atrocious bad weather and, after a 25-mile journey, reached the lightship.

Michael Higginbotham. Hero of the *Coningbeg* lightship rescue. (Jack Higginbotham)

The coxswain later told reporters,

> It was a terrible night, and when we cleared Carnsore Point we met the full force of huge Atlantic rollers, which smashed over the Lifeboat. We battered through the gale for over four hours before we succeeded in reaching *Coningbeg*. The lightship was rolling on her beam ends, and the seas were breaking all over her. I manoeuvred the life boat around her and made several attempts to go alongside on both the port and starboard quarters, but it was useless. If the lightship had struck us as she rolled into the trough we would have been stove in like an eggshell.[102]

The coxswain of the lifeboat later said that it was the worst weather he had ever encountered and that he had even considered abandoning any attempt to rescue the injured man.

Just as it looked like the injured man would have to wait for days to be taken off the lightship and rescued one of the crew, Michael Higginbotham volunteered to use one of the lightship's boats. He lifted the injured man into it and attempted to get to the lifeboat, despite the very heavy weather. This was a brave and desperate attempt to save the life of the injured man. The boat was swung out and the injured man lifted into it, with Michael Higginbotham getting back on board. The coxswain of the lifeboat said that as 'the lightship rolled downwards the tiny boat was lowered into the angry seas. Higginbotham paid out the line and allowed the boat to go astern. Huge waves tossed it about like a cork and half filled it with water, but by the flashing lantern we kept it in view, and when the little boat was clear of the *Coningbeg* I manoeuvred the life boat towards it, and after four attempts succeeded in picking it up.'[103] With great difficulty they managed to lift the injured man on board. The weather was so bad that there was no chance of Higginbotham getting back on board the lightship, so he was also taken on board the lifeboat and the lightship's small boat taken in tow. After a few minutes the little boat was swamped and lost. The lifeboat safely reached Rosslare and both men were taken to the local hospital in Wexford. Michael Higginbotham died in 1950.

The Higginbotham family had a long history of seafaring and working for the Commissioners of Irish Lights. The family lived in Parnell Street, an area of a south Wexford town where many seafaring families lived. Six of Henry Higginbotham's sons worked for the Commissioners of Irish Lights and Robert, who was just age twenty-three, was lost in the *Puffin* lightship disaster in 1896. Henry became Master of the *South Rock* lightship. He died in March 1921 on board from a heart attack. He was buried in Ballyphilip churchyard, Portaferry Northern Ireland, hundreds of miles from his home town. Three of Henry's sons also served on the lightships.

Henry Higginbotham

John Higginbotham

Above: Robert and Henry Higginbotham all had long service in the Irishlights. (Jack Higginbotham)

Left: Gravestone of Henry Higginbotham, who died on the *South Rock* lightship in 1921 and buried hundreds of miles from his family and friends. (Jack Higginbotham)

Since the first lights were manned, many individuals and crews of the Irish lightship service have been killed, injured or traumatised. Many others have lost their lives attempting rescues. These brave men were ill prepared for what happened, and it is no credit to the Irish nation that little or no recognition has been given for their sacrifice and the sacrifice of their families. No memorials have been erected to lightship men or medals struck by the nation to remember their bravery. A memorial trail and garden of remembrance to those lost at sea and the *Isolda* was opened on 17 June 2001 at Kilmore Quay, Wexford.

The last lightship in southern Irish waters, the *Guillemot*

Since the earliest times the *Coningbeg* lightship, placed near the Coningmore Rock and the half-submerged Coningbeg Rock, had a reputation as a dangerous station because of the tides, which move like great rivers, and the prevailing southerly and south-westerly winds. The rocks had been marked by a Trinity House lightship as early as September 1824. The lightship on this station was commissioned as a result of pressure from shipowners, underwriters and local authorities. The first vessel placed on the station was the *Seagull*, a wooden vessel built of oak, teak and elm planking. The *Seagull* was the first purpose-built lightship for the Irish Lights Commissioners. She had been built in 1823 by W. Roberts of Milford Haven at a cost £1,658, and in 1847 a large gong was substituted for the fog bell on this vessel to be used 'whenever the weather may be thick and foggy, so as to require such signal for the safety of shipping, a gong will be mounted on board.'

Lightships on this station were manned by eight crewmen, a Master, two lamplighters, two fog signallers and three seamen. They spent one month on station and one month off. In 1838 it was commented that the 'Saltee's light

A Notice to Mariners advising of the placing of a lightship on the Coningbeg Station in 1838. (Author's Collection)

NOTICE TO MARINERS.

NEW LIGHTS ON THE COAST of IRELAND.

THE Corporation for Preserving and Improving the Port of Dublin, &c. give Notice, that the under-mentioned LIGHT STATIONS will be Illuminated for the first time on WEDNESDAY, 1st of SEPTEMBER NEXT, and will continue to be lit in future from Sun-set to Sun-rise :—

CONINGBEG Floating Light Ship, situate off the Coast of Wexford; it bears by Compass N.E. ¼ E. from the great Saltee Island, distant 2¼ miles, 22 miles from Tusker Rock, W. ¼ S. from Coningbeg to Hook Tower, N.W. ¼ W. 14 miles.

The Vessel is fitted with three Masts, on two of which Lights will be hoisted.

vessel still rocks and pitches in every gale, so that the lantern is obliged to be lowered down nearly to her decks, and when is most wanted is rarely to be seen.'[104] The *Seagull* served for forty years before being withdrawn from station in 1854 and sold by auction.

Earlier, in January 1828, the *Coningbeg* lightship dragged her anchor nearly 5 miles. It was not until 24 hours later the tug steamer *Foyle*, of Dublin, was sent to tow her back to station. Again in September 1869 she dragged her anchor in a 'dreadful' storm and was driven from her moorings and carried out to sea. The station remained without a lightship for some days. In 18 September the Irish Lights Commissioners steamboat *Princess Alexandra* arrived at the south coast accompanied by the lightship *Gannett*, which was intended to replace the vessel that had been carried away in the storm two days earlier. It was two days before the weather allowed the *Gannet* to be placed back on station. In 1860s the *Coningbeg* station was provisioned by the *Petrel*, a Kilmore vessel of 14 tons, she was able to carry 25 tons and she cost new about £500.

The light of the *Coningbeg* was fixed and did not flash but this proved unsatisfactory and it was changed on the night of 10 September 1878, 'the light

A local boat, the *Petrel*, owned by Robinson's of Lightwater, Killinick, Wexford. She was used as the local tender to the lightships in the later 1800s. (Jack O'Leary)

on board the *Coningbeg* Light Vessel showing three flashes every minute in quick succession, the time occupied by the flashes being about 23 seconds; the interval of obscurity between each successive three flashes will be 37 seconds. The Light Vessel in the day time will be distinguished by having one mast and a jigger mast, the main mast having one ball at the masthead.' The colour of the lightship, like that of all other Irish vessels, was changed from black to red in 1955.

In June 1906 the White Star liner *Majestic*, sailing for Liverpool, miraculously escaped a head-on collision with the *Coningbeg* during a heavy fog. The collision was averted by the action of the captain. Because of the fog the steamer had been running at half speed and only sighted the lightship when about 15 feet away. The quick-thinking captain ordered the rudder put hard a-port, but the starboard side of the steamer grazed the *Coningbeg*. A panic by the passengers was reported but the steamer stopped and ordered boats to be lowered to ascertain if the lightship needed assistance but help was not needed. The accident happened despite the two vessels having been in wireless contact for some time. In 1925 a passing steamer reported that *Coningbeg* was sinking. The Wexford lifeboat was launched and put to sea but she returned hours later having not found the lightship in danger. In 1951 a new modern lightship equipped with wireless telegraphy was placed on this station. This vessel was equipped with wireless to communicate with other ships and shore stations.

In 1961 the *Albatross*, which was serving on the *Coningbeg* station, was replaced by a new vessel – the *Petrel*, which had been fitted with refrigeration and more comfortable accommodation. She was decommissioned in 1968. The *Gulliemot* which served on this station later was to become a maritime museum in Wexford harbour and Kilmore Quay for some years. She was sadly broken up some years ago and sold for scrap.

CHAPTER 15

The End of Manned Lightships

The economics of provision

The economics of the provision of the lightship service meant that by the middle of the twentieth century, their days as manned vessels were numbered. Technical developments meant that unmanned vessels were a possibility, and the majority of lightships were decommissioned during the 1970s and 1980s. All remaining lightships have now been converted to unmanned operation and most now use solar power. Many have now been replaced with light floats, or LANBY buoys or unmanned lighthouses which are vastly cheaper to maintain.

The first lightship to be replaced by an unmanned vessel was the *North Goodwin* on 22 April 1988. The *Inner Dowsing* was the last manned lightship in England and was replaced by a lighthouse in 1991.

Friday 26 March 1982 and Wednesday 31 March saw the demanning of the last two lightships in the Irish lights service. The *South Rock* and *Coningbeg* were taken off station. These were the last of the eleven lightships which had been placed about the Irish coast. The Chairman of the Irish Lights Commissioners, Sir William Blunden paid tribute to the last of the crews for the high standard of readiness of the vessels handed over. The last Master of the *South Rock* was Capt. C. Dumigan and of the *Coningbeg* Capt. S. Brennan.

The *Roaring Middle* light float, an automated replacement for the manned lightship. (Ian Simons)

The Coningbeg station was unmanned and automated on 24 January 1982. Its light then flashed white every 30 seconds and a radar beacon was installed. The unmanned lightship was finally replaced by a 'superbuoy', with a light that has a radius of 14 km. This buoy is fitted with automatic identification transponders, which are monitored at the Commissioner for Irish Lights headquarters in Dún Laoghaire.

Any romance is now gone. All lightships around the coasts of Ireland and the United Kingdom are automated and unmanned, which is why it is very important that the life and experiences of the brave men who manned these vessels should be told. Most who served have now died, and few remain to tell their courageous tales.

The last crew to serve on the *South Rock* lightship just before she was decommissioned in 1982. (Portaferry – *Past and Present*)

The *South Rock* after decommissioning in Dun Laoghaire Harbour, Ireland. (J Higginbotham)

References

1. Ballantyne R. M., *The Floating Light of the Goodwin Sands* (London: James Nesbit & Co, 1872). p. 12.
2. *San Francisco, California*, Vol. 83, No. 117, (California: 7 March 1898).
3. Kobbe, Gustav, 'Life on the South Shoal Lightship', *Century Magazine* (August 1891).
4. Golding, Captain Thomas (London: Smith & Ebbs, 1929) p. 794.
5. Ibid. p. 59c.
6. An Act touching Sea marks and Mariners Anno 8th Eliz. AD 1566.
7. 'Letter of the Duke of Ormond [Lord Lieut. of Ireland] to the Lord High Treasurer, respecting the lighthouses in Ireland', Joseph Redington ed. *Calendar of Treasury Papers*, Vol. 3, (London, 1874) p. 271–298.
8. PRO. Calendar of Treasury Books and Papers, Vol. 2 (1898) p. 33.
9. *Illustrated Guide Book: Isle of Wight* (London: Ward Lock & Co., 1948).
10. Hague, D. and R. Christie, *Lighthouses their Architecture, History and Technology* (Llandysul: Gower Press, 1974).
11. Golding, Captain Thomas (London: Smith & Ebbs, 1929) p. 11.
12. The Globe (London: 12 December 09).
13. Tarrant, M., *The Super Silent Service* (Llandysul: Gomer, 1998) p. 9.
14. 14. Whormby, J, *An Account of the Corporation of Trinity House of Deptford Stroud and of Sea Marks in General 1746* (Tower Hill, London: Smith & Ebbs, 1861) p. 8.
15. An Act touching Sea marks and Mariners Anno 8th Eliz. AD 1566.
16. Cotton, Joseph, *Memoir on the Origin and Incorporation of the Trinity House of Deptford Stroud* (London: J. Darling, 1818) p. 70.
17. Ibid. p. 3.
18. Barrett, C. R. B., *The Trinity House of Deptford Stroud* (London: Laurence & Bullen, 1883).
19. Cotton, Joseph, (London: J. Darling, 1818) p. 57.
20. Ibid. p. 31.

21. Harris, G. G., Ed., *Trinity House of Deptford 1609–35* (London: London Record Society, 1983) p. ix.

22. Le Gallienne, Richard, *Diary of Samuel Pepys Selected Passages* (Mineola, New York: Dover Publications Inc., 2012) p. 114.

23. Harris, G. G., Ed., *Trinity House of Deptford 1514–1660* (University of London: The Athlone Press, 1969) p. 146.

24. Golding, Captain Thomas, (London: Smith & Ebbs, 1929) p. 21.

25. Cotton, Joseph, (London: J. Darling 1818) p. vi.

26. Mead, H. P., *Trinity House* (London: Sampson Low, Marston & Co. Ltd, 1947).

27. Whormby, J., (Tower Hill, London: Smith & Ebbs, 1861) p. 6.

28. Storey, A., *Trinity House of Kingston Upon Hull* (Grimsby: Albert Gait Ltd, 1967).

29. Mason, J., *The History of Trinity House of Leith* (Glasgow: McKenzie Vincent & Co. Ltd, 1957).

30. Moir, David, R., *The Birth and History of Trinity House Newcastle-upon-Tyne* (Glasgow: McKenzie Vincent & Co. Ltd, 1958).

31. Cotton, Joseph, (London: J. Darling, 1818) p. 187.

32. *King's Lynn Corporation, A Calendar of the Freemen of Lynn 1292–1836* (Norwich: Printed for the Norfolk and Norwich Archaeological Society by Goose and Son Ltd, 1913).

33. Whormby, J., (Tower Hill, London: Smith & Ebbs, 1861) p. 134.

34. Ibid. p. 746.

35. Ibid. p. 131.

36. Ibid. p. 132.

37. Hamblin, R., *A Prospect Floating Light, Near to ye Buoy on the Nore Sand, etc.* (London: British Library, 1730).

38. *Caledonian Mercury*, Monday 26 July 1731.

39. Faultey, M. and J. Garon, *The Essex Coastline, Then and Now* (New Zealand: Potton Publishing, 2005) p. 208.

40. Trinity House History: Official history blog of the Corporation of Trinity House of Deptford Strond and its Lighthouse Service, INC., 1514 *Early problems with the Nore Lightvessel*, p. 745.

41. Whormby, J., (Tower Hill, London: Smith & Ebbs, 1861) p. 135.

42. Ibid. p. 137.

43. Ibid. p. 136.

44. Ibid. p. 139.

45. Ballantyne, R. M. (London: James Nesbit & Co., 1872) p. 54.

46. Ibid. p. 77.

47. Treanor, S. T., *The Log of a Sky Pilot: Or Work and Adventure around the Goodwin Sands* (London: The Religious Tract Society, 1893) p. 121.

48. Ibid. p. 120.
49. Tarrant, M., *The Super Silent Service* (Gomer: 1998) p. 36.
50. *Cornhill Magazine Light Vessels*, Vol. 111 (London: Smith, Elder and Co., 1861) p. 38.
51. Ibid, p. 38.
52. Treanor, S. T. (London: The Religious Tract Society, 1893) p. 131.
53. *Cornhill Magazine Light Vessels*, Vol. 111 (London: Smith, Elder and Co., 1861) p. 39.
54. 'On my Perch: Paul Roche Looks Back on his First Tour of Duty as a Temporary Light Shipman', *Beam Magazine*, No. 26.
55. 'The Sunday at Home', *Religious Tract Society*, Vol. 40 (1893).
56. Treanor, S. T. (London: The Religious Tract Society, 1893) p. 120.
57. Ballantyne, R. M., (London: James Nesbit & Co., 1872) p. 59.
58. Cook, A. O., *Life on a Lightship* (London: Hodder & Stoughton, 1915) p. 98.
59. *Hull Daily Mail*, Wednesday 31 January 1894.
60. 'A New Lightship for the Commissioners of Irish Lights', *Shipbuilding and Shipping Record* (April 1923).
61. *Slabline*, Issue 27 (Winter 1987) p. 12.
62. Tarrant, M., (Gomer: 1998) p. 44.
63. Carter, George, G., *Looming Lights* (Readers Union and Constable, 1945).
64. Rogers, John, D., 'Last Days of the Light Vessels', *Sea Breezes*, Vol. 63, No. 526 (October 1989).
65. Carter, George, G., (Readers Union and Constable, 1945) p. 54.
66. Ibid. p. 85.
67. Ibid. p. 106.
68. *Yorkshire Post*, Friday 2 February 1940.
69. *Glasgow Herald*, 9 February 1940.
70. Carter, George, G., *Looming Lights* (Readers Union and Constable, 1945) p. 132.
71. Carter, G., 'Goldsmith, Twixt Sand and Sea', *Leading Lights*, Vol. 1, No. 10 (Milford Haven: 1996).
72. 'Lighthouse Management', *The report of the Royal Commissioners on Lights, Buoys, and Beacons* (HMSO 1861).
73. *Sevenstones* lightship. Correspondence between F. Arrow and M. A. Smith (London: 1868).
74. *The Nautical Magazine* (Cambridge: Cambridge Library Collection, 1873) p. 319.
75. Tarrant, M. (Gomer: 1998) p. 38.
76. *Yorkshire Post and Intelligencer*, 19 March 1929.
77. *Dundee Evening Telegraph*, Wednesday 20 March 1929.

78. Baxter, R., *Sunday Express*, 5 July 1964.

79. *Morning Record*, 3 December 1966.

80. www.nlb.org.uk/HistoricalInformation/Ships/North-Carr-Lightship/.

81. Davenport Adams, W. H., *Lighthouses and Lightships: A Descriptive and Historical Account of Their Mode of Construction and Organisation* (London: T. Nelson and Sons, 1870) p. 29.

82. Ibid. p. 34.

83. Warburton, J., R. Whitelaw and R. Welsh, *History of the City of Dublin* (London: Cadell and Davis, 1818).

84. Blaney, J., 'Dublin Port and Ireland's First Lightship', *The Beam* (Dublin: 2008/09).

85. Warburton, J., R. Whitelaw and R. Welsh, *History of the City of Dublin* (London: Cadell and Davis, 1818).

86. *Morning Post*, 25 December 1821.

87. *Dublin Evening Mail*, Monday 24 September 1860.

88. *Wexford Independent*, September 1840.

89. Ibid. 24 January 1863.

90. Ibid. 15 August 1857.

91. *Wexford Independent*, 8 April 1865.

92. *The Freeman's Journal*, 5 April 1865.

93. *Wexford Independent*, 8 April 1865.

94. Letter in *The Times*, London 6 August 1864.

95. Hansard HC Deb. 21st January 1897.

96. Board of Trade Wreck Report for *Puffin* lightship, 8 September 1897.

97. Board of Trade Wreck Report for *Aigburth*, Formal Investigation into Accident, 1902.

98. 'Notice to Mariners', Ballast Office (Dublin: 9 April 1866).

99. *Northants Evening Telegraph*, Tuesday 9 September 1902.

100. *Northants Evening Telegraph*, Tuesday 11 September 1902.

101. *Wexford Free Press*, 28 September 1918.

102. *Leicester Daily Mercury*, 13 February 1939.

103. *Sheffield Evening Telegraph*, 13 February 1939.

104. http://www.carnsorechronicles.ie/page4.php.

Bibliography

The following have been used as sources in the writing of this book.

Books

A History of the County of York East Riding: Volume 1, The City of Kingston Upon Hull (London: Victoria County History, 1969).

Adams, Andrew, *Woodman, Richard, Light upon the waters The History of Trinity House 1514–2014* (London: The Corporation of Trinity House, 2013).

Allen, R, *Secretary Trinity House Letter to the Royal Society* (9 January 1873).

Armstrong, Warren, *White for Danger*, (New York: The John Day Comp., 1963).

Carter, George, G., *The Goodwin Sands* (London: Constable & Co. Ltd, 1953).

Chadwick, Lee, *Lighthouses and Lightships* (London: Dennis Dobson, 1971).

Collinson, Don, *The Dart Estuary Lights, Mark & Lighthouses* (Kingswear: The Kingswear Historians, 2004).

Colfer, Billy, *Irish Rural Landscape: Vol. 2, The Hook Peninsula* (Cork: Cork University Press, 2004).

Foley, M., *Disasters on the Thames* (Stroud: The History Press, 2011).

Grosvenor, J., *Trinity House* (London: Staples Press, 1959).

Hedges, A. C., *East Coast Shipping* (Oxford: Shire Publication, 1974).

Hore, Philip Herbert, *History of the Town & Country of Wexford* (London: Elliot Stock, 1906).

Harris, G. G., Ed. *Trinity House of Deptford 1514–1660* (University of London: The Athlone Press, 1969).

Information Leaflet Number 51: *Records of the Corporation of Trinity House* (City of London: London Metroplitan Archives, 2010).

Langmaid, K., *The Sea, Thine Enemy* (London: Jarrolds, 1966).

MacAlinden, B., *No Port In a Storm* (Latheronwheel, Caithness: Whittles Publishing, 1998).

MacAlinden, B, *Prisoners of the Sea* (Peter Williams Associates, 1999).

Major, Alan, *The Kentish Lights* (Seaford: S. B. Publications, 2000).

McCormick, W. H., *The Modern Book of Lighthouses Life Boats and Lightships* (London: A&C Black Ltd, 1936).

Meyrick, B., *Trinity House* (London: Sampson Low, Marston & Co., 1946).

Mudd, David, *Cornish Sea Lights* (Bodmin: Bossiney Books, 1978).

Nash, John, *Seamarks* (London: Stanford Maritime, 1985).

Phantom Ship Phantoms of the Sea (Waterford County Museum, unknown date).

Phillips, G. W., *Lighthouse and Lightship* (London: Robert Ross & Co., 1949).

Power, John, *A Maritime History of County Wexford Vol. 11 1911 to 1960* (Ireland: Olinda Publications, 2011).

Power, John, *Above and Beyond the Call of Duty* (Enniscorthy: C. & R. Print, 1993).

Price Edwards, E., *Our Seamarks* (London: Spottiswoode and Co., 1884).

Rees, John S., *History of the Liverpool Pilotage Service* (Southport: The Southport Guardian Ltd, 1929).

Russell, H., *The Longshoreman* (London: Sampson Low, Marston & Co., 1896).

Shakespeare, W., *The Merchant of Venice* (1605).

Sutton-Jones, K., *Pharos, The Lighthouse Yesterday, Today and Tomorrow* (Salisbury: Michael Russell, 1985).

Tarrant, M., *Cornwall's Lighthouse Heritage* (Truro: Twelveheads Press, 1990).

The Nautical Magazine (Cambridge: Cambridge Library Collection, 1873).

Woodman, Richard, *Keepers of the Sea* (Suffolk: Terence Dalton Limited, 1993).

Journals

Gibbs, R., 'The Trimming of the light Lamp', *Journal of the Association of Lighthouses Keepers* (June 1991).

Kelly, W. J., 'Irish Lights', *Sea Breezes* (1960).

Lane, A., 'Brake Lightship: A Story of Two Collisions Bygone Kent', Vol. 16, No. 6, *Meresborough Books* (1993).

Lane, A., 'The Last of the Lightship Men, Bygone Kent', Vol. 12, No. 10, *Meresborough Books* (1991).

Lane, A., 'Disaster on the South Goodwin, Bygone Kent', Vol. 13, No. 1, *Meresborough Books* (1991).

Lane, A., 'The Light Betwixt the Forelands Bygone Kent', Vol. 19, No. 4, *Meresborough Books* (1998).

Lane, A., 'Varne Lightvessel: A Channel Sentinel Bygone Kent', Vol. 24, No. 4, *Meresborough Books* (2003).

'Life on the New Shout Shoal Lightship', *The Century Magazine*, Vol. 42 (New York: The Century Company of New York, 1891).

'Light-Vessels', *The Cornhill Magazine*, Vol. 3 (London, 1861).

Rogers, John D., 'Last days of the Light Vessels', *Sea Breezes*, Vol. 63, No. 526 (October 1989).

San Francisco, California, Vol. 83, No. 117 (California: 7 March 1898).

Shrub, William, 'On the Gull Stream', *Coast & Country*, Vol. 10, No. 1 (Kent: Parrett & Nerves, 1981).

'The Lightship *Albatross* for the Commissioners of Irish Lights Engineering' (London: 7 and 21 January 1927).

'On this day 1745 Early Problems With the Nore Lightvessel', *Trinity House History* (Trinity House Board Minutes).

Wood, W., 'Life on a Lightship', *The Royal Magazine* (London: Pearson, 1899).

Woodward, D., 'The Accounts of the Building of Trinity House Hull, 1465–1476', *The Yorkshire Archaeological Journal*, Vol. 62 (1990).

Official reports

Board of Trade Wreck Report for *Newarp* Lightship and *Star of the Sea* (1855).

Extracts from the *Report of Her Britannic Majesty's Commissioners appointed to Inquire into The Condition and Management of Lights, Buoys, and Beacons* (6 March 1861).

Hansard HC. Deb., 17 February 1868.

Hansard HC. Deb. Vol. 132, March 1904.

'Notice to Mariners', *Ballast Office* (Dublin: 9 April 1866).

Redington Joseph, ed., *Calendar of Treasury Papers*, Volume 3, 1702–1707 (London: 1874).

Shaw, William A., ed., *Calendar of Treasury Books and Papers*, Volume 2, 1731–1734 (London: 1898).

Shaw, William A., *Calendar of Treasury Books*, Volume 19, 1704–1705 (London: 1938).

Newspapers

Dublin Evening Mail, 13 February 1860.

Dublin Evening Post, Tuesday 13 July 1824.

'Notice to Mariners', *Liverpool Mercury*, 12 December 1813.

'Notice to Mariners', *Liverpool Mercury*, 19 September 1814.

Northants Evening Telegraph, 9 September 1902.

The Free Press, 28 September 1918.

The Waterford Mail, 2 March 1867.
Western Daily Press, Friday 12 March 1930.
Wexford Independent, 16 December 1865.
Wexford Independent, 8 April 1865.
Wexford Independent, Wednesday 21 March 1866.